TO EARTH WITH A BUMP

*Dedicated
to my Family*

TO EARTH WITH A BUMP

Roger Spoor O.B.E.

The Pentland Press
Edinburgh – Cambridge – Durham – USA

© Roger Spoor, 1999

First published in 1999 by
The Pentland Press Ltd
1 Hutton Close
South Church
Bishop Auckland
Durham

ISBN 1-85821-544-7

Typeset in Minion by Carnegie Publishing,
Carnegie House, Chatsworth Road, Lancaster, LA1 4SL
Printed and bound by Bookcraft (Bath) Ltd

Contents

List of Illustrations

Author's Note

I AM GREATLY INDEBTED to many people who have assisted me in writing this book and encouraged me throughout the process.

Firstly, I am grateful to my cousin Robin Perry who helped to jog my memory of our childhood days. I am also particularly grateful to David Rogers, who was a patient with me at the Pinderfields Spinal Unit, for helping me to recall our time in the Unit, and for having provided a notable Postscript.

I am also grateful to Percy Cooper for helping me piece together my early days in the practice; to Brian Gillespie for reminding me of our days at Preparatory School; to Graham Grant for assisting me with the history of the Newcastle Council for the Disabled; to the late John Dornton for helping to get my thoughts on both Arthur Young and the Exmoor Calvert Trust into order; and to Steve Clark for reminding me about the South Tyneside Strategy Committee.

I am profoundly grateful to John Fryer-Spedding for agreeing to write the Foreword to this book which he has done with his usual generosity and perceptive wit.

My wife Sue has critically read every chapter in draft form and pulled no punches in telling me where alterations were required. She has helped materially to make it a complete book.

Finally, without the services of Jill Cole, my editor, the book would not have been completed so painlessly and effortlessly nor would the deficiencies in my grammar and expression have been corrected so admirably, to leave the book in its final state, which I hope proves a good read.

Foreword

HIS BOOK will make essential reading for anyone who has to learn to overcome a major reverse in life. The author might well have felt himself justified in borrowing Field Marshal Slim's title, "Defeat Into Victory".

On reading the book, the great 'what if' must necessarily arise. 'What if' the events in the Prologue and Chapter Five had not occurred? I know Roger well enough to say that, in that case, he would have gone to the top of his profession, as he has. He would have continued to be a sporting achiever, as indeed he remains. He would have given valuable voluntary service in the North East. And all this would have been against the setting of the happy family life which he has enjoyed. (It will be readily apparent that Sue has been such a key player in most of the events of this story).

So what is remarkable about this book? An accident causing disability does not make a different 'you'. You are the same person but the way in which you do many things will be different, often difficult, often very difficult. During the twenty four years for which Roger and I have been working together for the Calvert Trust, I have come to know a good number of disabled people who, like Roger, have 'gone to the top'. I have also known many disabled people who have devoted themselves to serving others with disabilities. There are, however, comparatively few who have done both. Roger has, and with such notable success. He has effectively fitted two lives into one. For a senior partner in a 'big eight' firm, there was little spare time. As a regular guest at Graham Park Road, I have learned the secret. Start early. Think and work fast. And always leave time to enjoy family life and your friends, to paint and to enjoy activities in the countryside. Perhaps reference to the occasional glass of port would not be inappropriate!

Roger is a natural leader. I have known many people say that he is 'irresistible', whether asking for voluntary service, money, or anything else. That is why so many organisations with which he has been associated have profited to such an extent. Disability has not changed this. It has, indeed, reinforced it. Roger has followed Leonard Cheshire's principle, set out in his book "The Hidden World": "We will find that it is in going out to help someone whose need is greater than ours that we solve our problems and become fulfilled ..."

Finally I must say that, as all his friends find him, Roger is essentially a person with a light heart and a great sense of humour. Certainly I have been privileged to share those for many years now. They bring with them a sense of joy which, as is evident in the following pages, prevails over many other sentiments. I am sure that readers of this book will themselves derive great pleasure from reading the story (to date) of Roger's life.

John Fryer-Spedding
(Founder of the Calvert Trust)
Cumbria, 1998

Prologue

E FELL ABOUT TWELVE FEET.

He fell with a crash that was loud enough to wake the entire household.

He lay still, not knowing whether he was alive or dead. He had no feeling at all, not even pain. He was conscious, but unwilling to wake up. He lay still, as if feigning sleep. He tried to think, but thoughts would not come to him. At last he tried to move. He found that he could not move.

Someone was talking to him. He began to speak, and found to his surprise that he could talk back. But nothing he said made any sense. He felt cold and knew that he was wearing only his pyjamas. Someone put a coat over him. They told him he must not move. He knew that he could not move.

After a time the ambulance came. Very gently, he was placed upon a stretcher. They put him in the ambulance and they gave him an injection and then the ambulance set off for the hospital.

Every jolt on the road sent pain coursing through his body. The journey felt as if it would last forever. Someone sat beside him, holding his hand. He was groaning with the pain which was now in his back. He asked for painkillers but they told him he had had enough. He stared up above, at the roof of the ambulance, concentrating on the pain, trying to understand it. How much longer could the journey take? The pain grew worse, and worse, and worse.

They arrived at the hospital. They took the stretcher out of the ambulance and put him on a large trolley. He groaned and asked for painkillers. They told him to be brave. The trolley rattled and jolted along many corridors and around many sharp corners. On one corner the trolley slid, sideways. He shrieked out aloud in agony and they shouted at him. At last they were in a lift, going up. It was quiet and peaceful.

They came to a Ward. Before they put him on a bed they gave him a sedative and then he lay still, looking up. The sedative had not worked. He was still conscious. Still aware of the pain. It felt as if his legs were tied down. He tried to move them, but there was no response. He tried to move his arms. Again and again and, slowly, he was able to lift them.

He pushed them gently into the air and then more widely. The pain was excruciating. He lay still.

Later the doctors came and gathered around his bed. They spoke in whispers to one another, as if he were not there. Some more doctors came, and looked, and then they all went away.

Later still one of the doctors came back, and spoke to him.

"You have broken your back. It is difficult, at this stage, to know how much recovery there will be. You will have to be very patient."

1

My Early Life

When does one first begin to remember?
Sir Winston Churchill

 HERE IS, I BELIEVE, a recognisable quality which charac-
terises certain geographical areas of the United Kingdom. In
the North East this manifests itself as a spirit of honesty and
determination – a willingness to survive against all the odds
and to take what chances life may throw at one. Although I have, in my
time, travelled all over the world I always relish the return journey, and
when the London train pulls gently over the River Tyne into Newcastle
Central Station I never fail to experience that familiar feeling in my gut
which tells me I am home.

My North Eastern roots stretch back some way. On the paternal side,
my grandfather John Joseph Spoor came from South West Durham, where
he ran a successful ironmonger's business and lived in Witton-le-Wear,
a small hillside village on the edge of the Durham coalfield. J.J. was a
well-respected figure both professionally and socially. A leading light in
the local Conservative Association, he travelled abroad extensively, in
particular to Canada, and was frequently called upon to lecture throughout Europe. But it was to the North East that he always returned. He had
a brother, my Great Uncle Ben. A lively and colourful figure and a
somewhat more active politician than J.J., Uncle Ben rose to become the
Labour MP for Bishop Auckland, serving as Minister for Finance in
Ramsay MacDonald's government. Alas, I cannot claim to have met either
of these paternal forbears. J.J. died in 1929, four years before I was born,
and although Uncle Ben survived rather longer, we were never introduced.
Wayward and unpredictable, he died from drink (so they tell me) in 1937.

J.J. was married three times, outliving all of his wives bar the last. My
father Kenneth was the result of this last union. In 1929, having qualified
in London as a Chartered Accountant, my father came to Newcastle to
work in practice with Jack Graham, who was later to become my godfather. The partnership of J C Graham & Spoor enjoyed moderate success

and when, in 1930, my father eventually married his sweetheart Dorothy Dickinson, he was able to provide her with a comfortable home in Benton, which was at that time a pleasant and undeveloped suburb of Newcastle.

My father had courted Dorothy Dickinson in South Lakeland, where a childhood of fresh air, physical exercise and horses had led her quite naturally to a career as a PT instructor. Horses were in her blood – her father James Dickinson had been Clerk of Cartmel Racecourse, and his father a trainer of some note. Mother was always a great sport and continued to enjoy all sorts of games, managing in her time to play hockey for no less than four counties. During their courtship they chased each other on their motor bikes through the Lake District, my father's missing thumb providing lasting evidence of his enthusiasm! I always felt hard done by when they would not allow me a motor bike when I was eighteen or so.

When I was born in 1932 it was thus into a reasonably well-off, comfortable, middle-class household. We had a car (a luxury at the time) and a maid who lived in. As an only child I was doted upon by my parents, and my childhood wanted for little. Sunny days, the tinny tune from the Eldorado Ice Cream man, wonderful summer holidays in the Lakes and my mother, endlessly patient, teaching me how to catch and hit a ball in our leafy suburban garden ... all of these form distinctly cheerful impressions of my earliest years. Of course one is rarely aware of happiness at the time it is enjoyed. At the tender age of three years some incident must have given me cause for distress for I took off on my tricycle one day, determined to leave home for good. Anxious parents eventually found their escapee some four miles away, none the worse for wear although somewhat doubtful as to the wisdom of his adventure. Another distinct early memory is that of being hit on the finger by a falling slate from the roof. I was bundled into the car and my mother drove me to the doctor's, holding with one hand my index finger which was hanging by a thread. Perhaps the episode is recalled so vividly not only because of its inherent drama but also because I bear the scar to this day.

By this time my father's mother, Granny Spoor, was living in Rockwood, a large, rambling house overlooking the estuary at Grange-over-Sands. Journeys to Grange form a vivid part of early memory, with the exceptionally long pull up Hartside announcing one's departure from the Pennines and entrance to the Lakes. We would always have to stop at the Helm Wind cafe perched on the top of Hartside, not only to admire the view of the Lakeland hills stretched out before us but also to allow the car to cool down. It was at Rockwood that I spent many early childhood holidays, and I have fond and vivid memories of dear Granny Spoor,

R.C.S., aged six.

white-haired, round-faced and sparkling with good humour, and her 'companion', a Miss Dugdale, who was known to me only as Auntie Kittie (although no relation). Breakfast was taken alone downstairs in the kitchen and then I would clamber back upstairs to find Granny, still abed, and climb in with her for a second breakfast!

Grange brought many delights, not least of which was the companionship of my cousin Robin. Two years older than me, Robin was the only child of my mother's sister Paul and her husband Len. They had, in former years, uprooted and emigrated to New Zealand, but the economies of sheep farming turned down badly and they returned to Grange. Auntie Paul was three years older than my mother and she and Len lived with Robin in the Dickinson family home, Heightside, which, whilst not quite as grand as Granny Spoor's, was nevertheless a comfortable house of generous proportion. I stayed there, sometimes with my parents, on so many occasions that I came to regard it as a second home. Auntie Paul could be stern, on the outside, but was as soft as could be on the inside She had a nut-brown, wrinkled face and she made a marvellous rice pudding! Quite often Auntie Paul and Uncle Len would arrange to meet my parents "half-way", often designating Alston or the Helm Wind cafe if it were open, in order to exchange either Robin or me, or some other body. But on some occasions there was no fixed rendezvous; they just kept going until they met. In those days there was little danger of missing each other. Just imagine trying to do it now!

I looked upon Robin as an elder brother and we spent hours together in the seemingly endless summer of childhood exploring the woods and hills around Grange. We were also allowed to play in the marvellous garden of the big house across the road (now the Methven Hotel) and on one occasion carried Robin's Hornby train set across and set it up on what had once been a lawn tennis court. Behind Heightside a field led through a wood and up a steep hill to a hospice. This building became, for Robin and me, a place of fantasy and magic, as we entered into a world of boyhood imagination: it was at once a castle, a fort and a dungeon and we would fight, rescue or capture one another with feats of bravery and derring do, as each game demanded. Deep in the woods was a newt pond, which Robin claimed gloriously as his own, and which he guarded jealously, I believe with his life.

For several years we would spend part of the summer with other family friends on a camping holiday at Rockcliffe, on the shores of the Solway Firth. My parents were leading lights of the group, which generally consisted of friends connected with Northern Rugby Club. This tradition began several years before the war and continued, briefly, after the war

Departure for Rockcliffe: Auntie Paul, Robin, R.C.S.

was over. There were always some of the party who were my own age, particularly Brian Gillespie and Sue and Jill Hodnett. Mother – unwilling to forsake her creature comforts entirely – would establish herself in a hut in the middle of the campsite, whilst everyone else slept in tents around. In late August 1939 I was staying as usual at Heightside, from where Auntie Paul took Robin and me to join my family at Rockcliffe. We set out from Grange in her red Morris Eight tourer with the hood down, carrying all the paraphernalia necessary for a beach holiday. I can remember claiming the privilege of the front seat as I was prone to car sickness at the time. We were excited at the prospect of all the usual delights of that shared camping holiday: bathing at Portowarren, mixed hockey on the sands and Harry Clapham playing the piano at The Anchor at Kipford, where the sailing boats were moored. This holiday, however, was to prove dramatically different from those that had gone before. For it was whilst we were at Rockcliffe that year that war broke out, and my father was called up. I was to see him only twice in the ensuing six years.

With the advent of the war, my time at the Lakes was extended, as my pre-prep school in Newcastle – Ackhursts – was evacuated to Penrith. I vividly recall the train journey from Newcastle, which was one of great excitement. Outsize gas masks hung around our infant necks but clearly we were oblivious to the inherent seriousness of the situation as we clambered aboard and then, much to the accompanying adults' consternation, enthusiastically proceeded to consume our entire food ration (intended to last us the whole day) even before the train had pulled out of Newcastle Central. As with much of life at the time, this was just one more good adventure.

During the years of the war and for some time afterwards, many of my school holidays were spent at Grange and, when petrol rations permitted, we would have long expeditions around the Lakes with some mountain climbing generally in prospect. Robin continued to climb throughout his life, conquering every peak in the Lake District. He now lives in Switzerland with his Swiss wife Liliane and still climbs all over the Alps. For a treat we would take a cruise on one of the Windermere steamers which were still in operation, such as *The Swift* or *The Cygnet*.

One especial remembered place is Humphrey Head, a popular picnic site which boasted a dramatic cave where, legend has it, the last wolf in England was cornered and killed. This was, for me, always a place of mystery. It was open at the top and one could look down into the depths where there was a narrow opening to the sea. The noise of the waves crashing and reverberating around the cavernous depths filled me with a sense of wonder and of awe. I also remember the great bore which would sweep across Morecambe Bay, in the days before the barrage was constructed. Those who knew the bay well could lead one across at low tide, but there was always the danger of quicksand – and of sinking without trace.

One day Robin and I went to a matinée performance of *The Wizard of Oz* at The Palace – Grange's only cinema. With the discerning eye of youth we both declared Judy Garland 'soppy', but Robin was fascinated by the tornado which had everything and everybody sailing through the air and apparently enjoying themselves! Perhaps this sowed the seeds of his interest in meteorology, a subject which he made his career.

In 1940 I had to move from Ackhursts to Newcastle Preparatory School, where some of my earliest and most lasting friendships were formed. John Fenwick, who went on to Rugby later to become Chairman of Fenwicks, Brian Gillespie, who went to Uppingham and then entered the world of stockbroking, John Douglass, who went to Sedbergh before me and became a lifelong friend and was my best man, Nigel Ward, John Ward, Kenneth Harrison and Jim White were just some of those contemporaries at NPS whom I have remained close to in later life. With the war still on, the school was evacuated some thirty miles north, to Eslington Hall near Whittingham, which is near the Cheviots in Northumberland. Holidays continued to be spent over in the Lakes, but it was at Eslington Hall that I was to spend most of my prep school years. Once again, it is a place of fond memories: of playing homeguards v paratroopers in the woods; of bicycle rides with Rhoda Cumberledge, the headmaster's daughter; and of the infamous Marcus Brackenbury, who made a bomb in Chemistry with the intention of blowing up the Masters' Common Room, escaped from the school, was found attempting to board an aeroplane and thereafter was never seen again! One of the masters was in charge of Gardening, and the boys were each given a small allotment to cultivate. I very quickly discovered that I had no aptitude at all for this particular pursuit, much to the despair of the master concerned. My strengths lay in other directions, however, and I thoroughly enjoyed my first taste of properly organised rugger, cricket and athletics. This was also to be the place where I first learned what hard work meant, as we were coached for our Common Entrance – the gateway to the public schools. Work and sport apart, my abiding memories of Eslington Hall are its grandness of scale, the vista from across the valley, its barn-like interior and the sweet coolness of moonlight air through the dormitory window at night.

NPS returned to Newcastle at the beginning of 1945, and I was immensely proud to gain my first fifteen colours that Spring Term. The last two terms of prep school were thus spent living at home which was, by this time, a flat around the corner from the school in Jesmond. With my father having been away since the outbreak of war, we had long since given up our house in Benton. Having joined the RAFVR before the war, father had volunteered for air crew at the age of 37 and had seemed to set to qualify as a navigator. However, it was decided that his eyesight failed to meet the required standard and he ended up as a Squadron Leader, spending the last two years of the war at Scapa Flow. Back at home, Mother contributed valiantly to the war effort, helping to keep father's office in reasonable shape and sitting it out on the roof to keep an eye out for the Germans, which resulted in her being awarded a medal for her services as a firewatcher.

During these last months at NPS I had two encounters with the medical profession. The first was a trip to see Professor Arckle, after I had complained of sore eyes. He examined my vision and then spoke to me solemnly. "Roger, I'm afraid I'm going to have to make you wear spectacles. But by the time you reach your fifties, my boy, you'll find you no longer have need of them – unlike the rest of us!" Since at the time it was impossible to conceive of ever reaching such a great old age this was very poor consolation for having to endure those ugly frames and suffer the scorn of my contemporaries. Professor Arckle was right, however, and his words still echo now, when I find my sight has adjusted naturally with age and I now only need glasses for long distance.

The second encounter was a somewhat more dramatic visit to hospital, with my first experience of real pain resulting in an emergency operation to remove an inflamed appendix. I recovered quickly, however, and with the Common Entrance under my belt (although without the Scholarship the school had anticipated I would achieve) I presented myself as a new boy at Sedbergh in September 1945. Since I had been away at boarding school for most of my Prep. School years, the prospect of Public School was not as daunting as it might have been. My mother drove me over on the first day of term, any concerns of her own allayed, I suspect, by the fact that my prospective Housemaster, Len Taylor, happened to be a close family friend. My early confidence was shaken somewhat with my intro-duction to 'fagging'. Brian Braithwaite-Exley was my Head of House, and also Captain of Rugger. This gave him the status of a god ... and I was his minion, at his every beck and call. I had to clean his boots and shoes, press his trousers, run all his errands, prepare his tea and wash up after the huge feasts indulged in by the prefects in their studies, after we younger boys had gone to bed. Fagging, however, was a part of the school tradition. All boys endured it in their first year, but quickly progressed to the comfortable anonymity of middle school. Fagging is not to be confused with bullying; the prefects were rarely unreasonable in their demands and although there may have been some subtle 'manoeuvring' by one or two who took advantage of their power, it must be said that the school was generally a happy one.

Sedbergh provided the foundations for some firm friendships: Terry Gilmour, Colin Crabtree, Sam Toyne, Zeke Smith and John Benson were all contemporaries of mine who remained good companions as our aca-demic careers progressed. We were in Evans House, the oldest House in the school. The building was a bit of a rabbit-warren but we were proud of it and proud, too, of Len Taylor who kept us all in line and whose bark was much worse than his bite. Colin Crabtree and I invented our own version of fives cricket, which we played endlessly in the derelict fives court in our yard. On half day holidays, Colin, John, Terry and I would go swimming in the flat rock pools of the River Lune. There are other fond memories: of skating on Lillymere during the hard winter of 1947; of water colour painting expeditions to Baugh Fell with the Head-master (the legendary Bruce-Lockhart) or my House Tutor, Dick Pentney; of falling in love with one of the maids; and of going out to high tea with my mother when she managed to get over to see me and would feed me and a whole host of my chums. Colin Crabtree's parents also visited and would take us all off to their cottage, which was half way between Sedbergh and Casterton, where we were fed sumptuous picnics and permitted to swim in the river. There were several unofficial visits to the cottage, too, as it proved a highly convenient location to meet the girls from Kirkby Lonsdale. In the Summer Hols. we dispersed, although Terry Gilmour and I embarked on cycling expeditions together in Scotland. We would stay in Youth Hostels and spend our days cycling or walking for miles, or mountain climbing, conquering peak after peak with boundless energy.

My chums and I had a lot of fun together at school and were not averse to breaking the rules now and then – on one occasion this meant being discovered out of bed on the last night of term by an enthusiastic prefect and on another being caught smoking by an over-zealous padre. The punishment for smoking was a beating by the Headmaster although, in fairness, we were generally offered an alternative, which was to produce a six page essay. I confess I generally opted for the beating.

Sport featured strongly at Sedbergh and I was always a willing partici-pant. The school motto was 'Dura Virum Nutrix' (stern nurse of men) – a maxim carried out to the letter through the regime of cold baths every morning and shorts being compulsory dress, even in the winter – with the exception, of course, of Sundays when we had to wear grey flannels for Church. Running over the fells, rugger, cricket, tennis, squash and fives were daily activities and I took part enthusiastically, if not outstand-ingly. Being quite tall I had outgrown my strength and my level of co-ordination left something to be desired. Consequently I was a much better athlete at twenty three than at seventeen. However, I had my mother's training behind me and my good eye for a ball, coupled with my long reach, gave me natural advantages. Fives was always my best game.

One of the great sporting traditions at the school was the ten mile run, known as The Wilson Run. In this, the toughest of races, I recall running alongside Tom Cones, who was then Head of School House. Tom helped me up the treacherous Muddy Slide and over the tangled heather of Baugh Fell, while I paced him back from Danny Bridge with my longer stride. Ties were not officially encouraged in this race, but we breasted the tape together since we had clearly helped one another throughout the run and we finished equal twenty-ninth (out of sixty two).

I worked reasonably hard but was never terribly excited by academic study in the earlier years. Maths was always quite a strong point and I would dabble in Chemistry but Physics was a dead loss – much to Len Taylor's despair. In my GCE year the school was hit by an outbreak of infantile paralysis, which swept through the school and affected many of the boys. One boy died and two were badly paralysed and eventually it was decided to close the school early that summer term. This caused problems for many of the boys whose parents were abroad, including my friend Sam Toyne. My parents generously agreed that Sam could come home with me. GCE papers were sent to respective homes and Sam and I sat our formative exams in the rather cramped surroundings of my father's office, with one of the partners of the firm invigilating.

My GCE results were surprisingly good and with these under my belt my academic confidence increased. At last I had risen enough to be granted admission to the dizzy heights of Clio, the English and History Upper Sixth at Sedbergh. Clio was housed in the subdued grandeur of the original school building where we worked without much supervision in the musty interior of the library. There was always an air of superiority surrounding those who inhabited Clio and once I was among their number I began to understand why. Separate from the hurly burly of the lower and middle school, here one could begin to understand and appreciate the pleasure of real learning. One was respected not only by one's juniors but by the masters, too. I recall one memorable hot summer's afternoon: we had relinquished our studies and gone outside for a game of Clio Cricket (our own version of the game) when much to our dismay the Headmaster suddenly appeared. Guiltily we stopped playing but instead of chastising us he asked if he could join in.

After two more intense years of school work I was rewarded by pretty good Highers results (the equivalent of 'A' Levels) and, much to my parents' delight, also passed the scholarship examination to Cambridge. Destiny, however, had other plans.

My years at Sedbergh had taught me to fight my own battles and to stand on my own two feet. I had learnt to live with my mistakes, be cheerful at all times and above all to strive to get the utmost out of life. I emerged from my school years with a reasonably good academic brain. My body was still disproportionate in height and strength but I was supremely fit and had acquired a taste for most sports. Perhaps my only regret was that I did not learn to fish, although this was a skill I was soon to acquire and enjoy for many, many years ahead.

Sedbergh also left me with an abiding love of the Fells, with their deep romantic ghylls and sparkling streams. The dramatic outline of Winder, the hill which stands guardian-like over the school, is an image which all Sedberghians keep with them throughout their lives. I was about to embark on a path that was to shape my life ahead. But I had not yet given myself any serious challenges. I had accepted life as it came along, sometimes reacting quite well, at other times perhaps not so well, but without any particular design or purpose. I had still to learn that if you are to achieve anything in life, then the first step is to set yourself some goals.

2

An Articled Clerk

The grettest Clerkes been noght wisest men.
Geoffrey Chaucer

HERE WERE TWO REASONS for not taking up my place at Cambridge. Whilst still at Sedbergh I had, naturally, given considerable thought to the future and it seemed to me logical that a good professional qualification would stand one in good stead. My father's practice provided an excellent model; a sound financial business training which would ultimately offer the choice of staying in the profession or of moving into industry if one so wished. I had been working at full stretch in the summer of 1950 (my final year at Sedbergh) for my examinations and it occurred to me that if I were to consider sitting further exams I had better do so whilst I was still young and adaptable. Thus the accountancy profession beckoned, although when I made the decision to train I had certainly not made up my mind that this might be a career for life.

The second reason was that in 1950 National Service was still in force, and I was determined to serve my time in the Royal Navy. However the RN was very selective and in effect one had to prove one's enthusiasm and dedication first. The only sure way to do this was to have some sort of a track record in the Naval Reserve. I therefore decided to apply to have my National Service deferred until I had completed my Articles of Clerkship and qualified as a Chartered Accountant and at the same time serve in the RNVR.

Thus it was that I set my sights on the first two major goals in my life – to qualify as a Chartered Accountant and to become an officer in the Royal Navy. It helped me over the next five years to keep reminding myself of these goals.

I joined the RNVR by enrolling as an Ordinary Seaman in *HMS Calliope*, one of the oldest wooden-walled steamships with a great history, which was moored alongside Vickers Armstrong on the Tyne. I did this a few days before I embarked upon my training as an Articled Clerk. I was articled to John Crisp, Senior Partner of a small Newcastle firm called Percy F Ward & Co. although for the first few months there was no vacancy for me there and I worked in my father's firm under the guidance of his great friend and partner Percy Cooper. Later I would be proud to become their partner in the family firm.

Five years' articles has been likened to a prison sentence and it certainly was a long slog, but in those days we were only paid a little pocket money and we did not work at the pace or pressure that today's accountants have to maintain as students for months on end. Because of my father's friendship with John Crisp I did not have to pay a premium for my articles, which was customary in those days. I would be sent out on audit as assistant to a senior clerk and we would normally spend up to four weeks at a clients' premises, working through our audit programme and arriving at the end with an audited Balance Sheet and Profit and Loss Account that told the story of the client's business for the previous year. Sometimes we were not on a tight timetable and we would have time to meet other clerks in town for coffee on the way to work. That doyen of unqualified seniors, Joe Swinburn, believed in the social side of auditing and frequently led me astray, but he was very conscientious on the job and I remember once spending three weeks with him looking for a difference of two pence in a trial balance.

One of the benefits of not having too strenuous a working day was that it left you in better shape for swotting in the evening. During the five years of articles you had to sit and pass an intermediate examination after about two and a half years and a final examination at the end of your articles. You would be given study leave for up to three months before the exams and I actually attended a three month course run by Foulks Lynch in London before my final; although I think I would have passed without this heavy swotting it was a sort of insurance. The main work however, was conducted through a series of correspondence courses which covered the entire syllabus for each examination and lasted for most of one's articles. I set aside three nights a week to work, increasing this as the examinations drew nearer and using weekends to catch up if I fell behind. Every Monday evening belonged to *Calliope* – so there were not many to spare!

During this time I lived at home with my parents, who were both extremely supportive. My father gave me a small allowance and I had a study to myself where I worked. Some of the work was extremely interesting, but quite a lot was routine learning and just hard work. It helped, of course, if you could get interested in the subject and two of the aspects that did interest me in particular were Company Law and Share Valuations. There seemed few, if any, questions in my final examination on

Father and mother.

either subject! I was able to work quickly with figures and this aptitude helped me to answer examination questions within the time frame allowed. I was placed in the first hundred out of well over a thousand sitting the intermediate and this gave me confidence that I would be able to pass my final examination first time. This I was determined to do: I had a future appointment to keep with the Royal Navy!

Of course all work and no play never did anyone any good. Apart from my sacrosanct Monday evenings I therefore permitted myself time for sport and socialising and managed to live life pretty much to the full. I never worked on a Saturday, when I played rugger and squash in the winter and tennis or cricket in summer. Northern Rugger Club played a significant role, and in 1951/52 I captained the 3A XV, a young side from which players would expect promotion to the second and first XVs. My mother acted as my match secretary and we often had to card a lot more than fifteen players because we knew that we would lose them to teams higher up. Her best resource was the Potts Family from mid-Northumberland. Each Saturday Mrs Potts would ring her up to ask her how many sons she needed that day. She had five! In spite of this peculiar manner of selection we were extremely successful, remaining unbeaten throughout the season, and winning the Northumberland Junior Cup without a point being scored against us. I made a rule that on Saturday nights it was not *de rigueur* to leave Northern if guests were to be entertained, and girls, therefore, were only tolerated much later in the evening!

Not that I had anything against girls. Within the constraints of available income I would invite different girlfriends to dances or out to dinner. It was on one such "later" Saturday evening that I first met Susan Daniels, who was with John Douglass at the South Northumberland cricket club dance. *Inter alia*, I used to take out Valerie Clements who eventually married John, whilst I was destined to marry Sue. Sometimes we would all end up in Peter Chen's new Chinese Restaurant in Northumberland Street, "The Maykway", to provide blotting paper to mop up the beer we had drunk at Northern. Tilleys restaurant was one of the institutions in Newcastle in those days and occasionally I would dine there with my parents and other friends in the old fashioned atmosphere, enlivened by the three piece orchestra on the mezzanine floor above. My twenty-first birthday party was held in the upstairs ballroom.

The captains of the Northern 1st and 2nd XVs respectively were George Gibbs and Ben Crowdy. George and Ben taught me how to play Bridge for money and many an evening was spent in George's digs with a case of beer, learning in a very hard school. George happened to live next door to Susan Daniels.

My mother was keen to see that my tennis should be improved and she arranged for me to have lessons from a professional of the Northumberland Lawn Tennis Association, Mr Evans. He did his best with me, but the highlight of my tennis career was playing in the semi-final of the open doubles in the Northumberland Annual Championship with Tommy Hodgson, against two county players from Middlesex. We reached 6/6 in the first set before my erratic serve let us down and we sank without trace. I suspect I had more talent for cricket. I started playing cricket for County Club but David Nelson, who was an articled clerk like me, persuaded me to play for Humshaugh in the West Tyne league. This was village cricket at its fiercest. Joe Bell was our groundsman. He was also the local poacher, special constable and our umpire! If David and I wanted to get away early to a party Joe would see to it that the opposition's wickets tumbled. One day I took a team from Newcastle to play a friendly against Humshaugh and included one or two good cricketers like George Gibbs. Most of the team, however, just came for the fun: Brian Gillespie, John Douglass and Michael Marchbank among them. We had a very merry day and a splendid party in the pub afterwards.

In 1952 I joined the Committee of the Northern Society of Chartered Accountants Student Society and played a role in organising students' activities. I began to feel more comfortable speaking in public and making my point of view felt in Committee or Open Forum. Student Societies are natural talking shops and we all relished the opportunity to talk knowledgeably about a great variety of subjects without much practical experience of any of them.

One year my friends John Douglass and Malcolm Sadler and I decided to have a holiday on the Norfolk Broads. We hired a Bermuda-rigged boat, which slept three comfortably, and met together at Great Yarmouth. We were all accountants or trainees, all played for Northern and together were like the three musketeers.

That holiday provided plenty of adventures, including ramming a Police launch. One time I was in the dinghy and the boat was in a narrow canal, coming at me quite fast. John passed me an oar, but such was the speed of the boat that I was swept out of the dinghy and got a ducking. It took us some time to retrieve our dinghy. Another boat with several girls on board seemed to frequent the same pubs as we did and we got the distinct impression that they were chasing us. I dare say that they may have thought the opposite. On another occasion we were tacking against wind and stream with Malcolm pushing with the aid of the dinghy's out-board motor and with John at the helm. I was below preparing lunch when I heard a crash and an ominous sort of glugging noise. I came on deck to find an apologetic John attempting to mollify the irate owner of a motor boat who stupidly had strayed across our path and allowed John to hit and sink his dinghy. I kept a diary of our holiday which was variously entitled "Three Men in a Boat", "The Saucy Sue" or "Gorgeous Gwenda" and it caused endless hilarity whenever it was brought out and one of our number was present to remember the many different incidents.

Whilst at Sedbergh I had been introduced to skiing. The White family had invited me to join them in Switzerland one Christmas holidays, and I immediately fell in love with the exhilarating white clad mountains and this dramatically exciting sport. After the mandatory twenty or so falls on my first morning of instruction I got on quite well and passed my Third Class Ski Club of Great Britain examination that year. Skiing off piste and creating fresh tracks in virgin snow was my great delight. In the winter of 1953/54 I decided that a skiing party would be a good idea and organised a group to ski at Lech, in Austria. Most of us were from Newcastle, including Sue Daniels, but Terry Gilmour from Sedbergh and my cousin Robin were also among the party. Bill Hart, an old family friend, and Mig Wardle from Newcastle had not met before. It was on that skiing holiday, however, that they fell in love and, much to my satisfaction as a matchmaker, were eventually married.

We had quite severe winters in the North-East in those years, and on more than one occasion I remember skiing to the office which was at the bottom of the city, all downhill. By 5 o'clock, however, all the snow would have melted and I would have to carry my skis home on the trolley bus, which generated some most peculiar looks from my fellow passengers. In really hard weather we were able to ski in Northumberland and in the Pennines, but to get there in those days we had to fit chains because snow ploughs did not operate very far out of town and the roads would be treacherous. Lower temperatures in those days also gave us frozen lakes which led to skating and Town versus Country ice hockey matches. One New Year's Eve there was heavy snow and a big party planned at Northern. Undaunted, I donned my skis and set off for the party where I had a thoroughly good time. At the end of the evening I set off again into the night, gliding home through the deserted streets of Newcastle via the houses of various acquaintances who were more than a little surprised to be 'first-footed' by a visitor on skis.

John and Malcolm and I used to run together on training runs round the Town Moor on Monday evenings and we would generally find an excuse to call at the home of one or more girls on the way. I went out with a lot of different girls to parties, dances and hunt balls. Lalage Swinburne ran a dance club at Hexham called the Terpsichoreans to which Sue and Val and John and I were regulars. By the time the end of my articles was in sight I had set my self another goal. I was determined to marry Sue Daniels and when she accepted I was the happiest man in Newcastle. We became engaged in June 1955 just after I had sat my final examination and completed my articles, and planned to be married in October 1956.

In Malta.

3

At Sea

They sailed away for a year and a day ...
Edward Lear

N MOST MONDAY NIGHTS and occasionally on a Wednesday, throughout the full five years of articles, I found my way down Scotswood Road, to *HMS Calliope*. When I enrolled in the RNVR I was given the rate of Ordinary Seaman, which was, in status, pretty much the lowest rung of the Royal Navy. There was a healthy cross section of social classes on *Calliope*, with a particularly strong artisan engineering representation which obviously reflected the industrial background of Tyneside. Although there was a sprinkling of potential officers in our number there was very little evidence of class distinction, and those Monday evenings provided a marvellous opportunity to meet and make good friends with several ship mates whom I would not have encountered in my ordinary social life.

At the beginning of the evening we would fall in for divisions and then spend the time under instruction, in lectures on practical seamanship, drilling or, on summer evenings, either sailing or pulling on the river. We had our own tender, later appropriately called *HMS Northumbria*, a coastal class mine sweeper, and most of our practical instruction was in *Northumbria*. Once or twice I would spend a weekend in *Northumbria* and every year my Principal permitted me 14 days' sea training. This would either be in *Northumbria* or with the Fleet. I can remember spending a fortnight in the *HMS Duke of York* based in Portsmouth. *Duke of York* was a huge Battleship and I can recall the size of the gigantic guns, scrubbing decks, painting ship and, when we had finished, the wonderful scale of the quarterdeck with its newly scrubbed teak deck and gleaming brasswork.

In the winter of 1951 King George VI died and volunteers were called to line the route of his funeral in London. I put my name down and thus attended my first parade of any significance. I remember it being extremely cold and wet. My position was in the Mall, and we stood to attention, then rested on our arms reversed as the cortege passed by on its way to the Abbey.

The following year I volunteered once again for formal duties – this time to line the route for the Coronation of Her Majesty Queen Elizabeth. This was a much more ceremonious occasion and we were drafted to Chatham Barracks for several days square bashing beforehand to make sure we were in good shape. The officers were given even more intensive training than the ratings and I remember thanking my lucky stars I was not being kept in for extra drill one evening when I came up to London to attend a debutantes' ball – altogether much more fun! Came the great day and it rained. We were in position in Whitehall several hours before the Royal Procession came past. The white blanco from our caps and belts dripped and ran down our faces and over our uniforms, wasting all our detailed preparations for the parade. Nevertheless I had a wonderful view of the Royal Procession. That evening I went to one of the special coronation parties and I had to change out of my bell bottoms into evening dress. I had left the latter in the left luggage department at Kings Cross station and there I repaired to have a bath after we were dismissed. The attendant in the subway bathrooms was somewhat astonished to see the matelot who had entered his bathroom emerging dressed in white tie and tails!

I performed one other parade duty of significance in my time on the lower deck. It was traditional on Armistice Day for each service to act as sentry at one corner of the Cenotaph which stands in Eldon Square in Newcastle. One year I was asked to be the Naval sentry. The required drill is complex and we had to undergo a lot of coaching not only learning the right movements but also learning how to keep absolutely still for nearly an hour. But it was great fun to be part of such an impressive ceremony. We were rewarded by seeing our pictures in the paper the next morning and watching ourselves on Pathé News.

HMS Calliope was a wonderful old ship, one of the earlier power driven corvettes in the Fleet, of the Comus class. She was 235 feet long with a displacement of nearly 2800 tons and when in service had a complement of 280 officers and men. She was commissioned in 1887 and in March 1889 she was in New Zealand attached to the Australian Station. She was sent to Apia harbour in Samoa where there was trouble ashore with rival chiefs claiming sovereignty and being supported by Germany and USA respectively, with Britain keeping a generally neutral stance. Apart from some merchant shipping there were three US and three German warships in the harbour when Calliope arrived and on the evening of the 15th March a terrible hurricane hit Apia Bay, causing utter chaos. In the midst of the storm *Calliope* got up steam, slipped her storm anchors and threaded her way through the maze of drifting powerless vessels to get out to open sea. All the other ships were sunk or beached with serious loss of life and the fine seamanship of Captain Kane and the crew of *Calliope* has forever after been praised in the annals of British naval history. To have a ship with such a history for an RNVR HQ was a great inspiration to the officers and men of Tyne Division and we were very conscious of our responsibility. Each year the officers dine to remember *Calliope's* escape from the hurricane and one of the junior officers tells the tale in his own words. I was to have my turn in due course.

As the years of my articles rolled by I was advanced in the RNVR to Able Seaman, and then to Leading Seaman, when I qualified as mine sweeper second class (the primary role of the RNVR was to provide a number of mine sweeping crews to the reserve).

When I had at last taken and passed my final Chartered Accountancy examinations I was given a date to join the Royal Navy for my National Service. It seemed that my first two goals were now attainable and it was with not inconsiderable excitement that I travelled down to Portsmouth to report to Victoria Barracks. I was earmarked as a potential officer (upper yardman) for which my five years on the lower deck as a seaman should have stood me in good stead. Sadly, however, my eyesight let me down – as my father's had many years before in his career with the RAF. My sight had deteriorated quite rapidly with the intensive swotting for my final examinations and I had no choice but to transfer to the Supply and Secretariat branch. It so happened that the Base Supply Officer in Portsmouth was Rear Admiral Laurie Boutwood, a cousin of my mother, and he invited me to dine with him while I was awaiting my officers Selection Board. He took a keen interest in my brief naval career and it may not have been a complete coincidence that I finished up in the Mediterranean, which was where I had asked to serve.

But first there was Hood Term: four months intensive officers training at *HMS Ceres* at Wetherby, opposite the racecourse where all budding Supply and Secretariat officers were put through it. I had never been so fit in my life! We were made to run everywhere, play rugger three times a week, constantly working and playing so that sleep became a distant memory. One weekend Sue came to see me and provided a gentle leavening from my diet of male toughness. Several of us had tea with her in her hotel and she remarked that it was like entertaining a bunch of schoolboys! In the spring of 1956 I passed out of Hood Term and was commissioned as a Probationary Temporary Acting Sub Lieutenant RNVR – as Ludovic Kennedy once said you can't get much lower than that! Some of my contemporaries in Hood Term were Accountants and Lawyers but two, surprisingly, went into the Church. I had rather lost touch with all of them except Jeremy James, who was a mutual chum of Derek Bradbeer. However we recently had a most enjoyable reunion in London and met old friends we had not seen for forty-two years!

My first appointment was to the First Submarine Squadron in Malta. Before leaving England I made my first serious financial investment. With the aid of a deposit from my father and a dormant loan on mortgage from the Marine & General with a life policy I was able to buy our first house. Number 3, Rectory Terrace, Gosforth was a solid and quite handsome mid-Victorian terrace house. It was all very exciting, the only minor worry being the fact that I had no money to service the mortgage. However, I possessed the confidence of youth and it was with a great sense of optimism that in April 1956 I duly departed for the Med. and, once in Malta, reported for duty in *HMS Forth,* the depot ship of the Squadron.

Sue's father had spent the entire war in the Royal Navy and had just retired in the RNVR as a Surgeon Captain in *Calliope.* I was honoured to be given his officer's tin trunk, his sword and a mess undress uniform. The latter I had to have taken in twelve inches and also had to remove, carefully, seven stripes from each sleeve, replacing them with my solitary Sub Lieutenant's stripe. Thus equipped, however, I felt ready for anything. It was warming up in Malta and almost immediately we went to whites. I was most anxious to see life in a submarine and fairly soon I got the opportunity, when I was asked to go to sea for a day in *HMS Sentinel.* I thoroughly enjoyed the excitement of my first day in a submarine (although we did not dive) and familiarised myself with the layout of the decks and beyond. Thus began a relationship that lasted throughout my whole time in Malta.

In *Forth* I was made Deputy to the Deputy Supply Officer and went round gaining experience of the different departments. Some of my time was spent in the Captain's office working with the Captain's secretary, which I found most instructive. One of the duties of Scratch (the Secretary) is to be the interpreter of Queens Regulations and Admiralty Instructions (QR & AI), which is the Bible of the Royal Navy. The Captain relied on his secretary enormously and in turn he taught me a great deal.

History was to repeat itself with an outbreak of infantile paralysis which had claimed a young life at Sedbergh. Although this epidemic was not nearly as serious as the one which had raged at school we did have one or two cases on board and the instruction came to sail away from Malta. Reluctantly *Forth* departed and after some time finished up in Cyprus where General Grivas happened to be making a bit of a nuisance of himself at the time. The Royal Marines who were stationed at Limasol entertained us in a most hospitable fashion before taking one or two of us on patrol in the mountains to search for Grivas and his terrorists. It was extraordinarily hot and we were not as fit as the Marines. The cliffs and mountains of Cyprus soon found out our weaknesses.

Back in Malta, sport seemed pretty high on the Navy's agenda and there was a lot of rugger (on very hard ground), and cricket. There was also a very sporting nine hole golf course at the Officers' Club at Marsa.

On one occasion Martin Wemys, the Commanding Officer of *Sentinel*, asked me to join them for an exercise. Of course I accepted eagerly. This time the submarine was submerged for most of her time at sea, which I had not experienced before. I was amazed at how quiet and peaceful it was after the rolling pitch on the surface. We slept around a square table, double bunking with some of us on watch, and I was most grateful for being accepted by *Sentinel's* officers into this strange world. Ken Frewer, who was the First Lieutenant, Terry Thomson, Alastair Bruce, Doyne Nicholson and Chris Belton have all become lifelong friends.

Back in *Forth* I completed my time with a different set of supply responsibilities, including galley duty. One of my duties was to taste the dinner being prepared for the ship's company. It was not bad but standards have improved vastly over the last forty years.

It was the summer of 1956, and the threat of Colonel Nasser at Suez was building rapidly. Among others, the Third Battalion of the Coldstream Guards was mobilized and sent to Malta. The Battalion comprised mainly reservists: accountants, lawyers and other professional people from the city. Upon arrival on the island they proved a most gregarious lot, wont to give splendid parties. The submariners by this time had a firm base on Malta and were already well entrenched in the island's social round. The Grenadier Guards quickly realised that they would need an ally to infiltrate the bastions of society and thereby gain access to all the eligible girls. We appreciated that we were merely being used as go-betweens but could not complain as our social lives improved dramatically!

Sue and I had planned to get married in the October, but it seemed as the time approached that world events (the Suez war rumours) were massing against us. As the intended day drew nearer I plucked up the courage to ask my Commanding Officer for permission to return to the United Kingdom for our wedding. He looked at me sternly and, assuming that my plans were to be dashed, I cabled Sue in haste. Eventually, however, the matter appeared on the agenda for the Monday morning meeting of the Gang of Four. These were the four Admirals who, headed by the Governor, Admiral Sir Guy Grantham, ran Malta. The provisional date Sue and I had set was October 6th. Poor Sue was on tenterhooks and close to despair when I sent a second telegram announcing that I had a 96 hour pass. The preparations which had been in suspended animation were immediately pressed in to action.

On Wednesday 3rd of October I was in *Sentinel* off the coast of Sicily. We anchored off Taormina that evening so that the officers of *Sentinel* could take me ashore for the first of my stag parties. I don't remember much about it but I do remember sleeping most of the following day as we returned on the surface to Malta. That evening I had another stag party with as many of the Squadron Officers as could take part. The next day I was taken to Luqa airport from where I hitched a lift with a friendly Flight Lieutenant on an RAF plane to Heathrow. I then had to pay for a flight up to Newcastle. It was one of the first flights of the Viscount and the stewardess bet me that a threepenny bit (the octagon) would stand up on the windowsill during take off. It did! The journey had seemed interminable but once home I greeted my bride-to-be who had remained superbly calm and I knew at once that it had all been worthwhile. My Newcastle friends had been waiting impatiently to celebrate and I endured my third (and final!) stag night.

We were married at Jesmond Parish Church and the reception was held in the Old Assembly Rooms. A guard of honour was provided by various naval friends and officers from *Calliope*. Sue's sister Jane and Lalage Sadler were our bridesmaids. The usual tricks were played on us at the end of the wedding and I was manhandled down the staircase by my old rugger pals, but we fooled everybody by going north and spending our first night at The Blue Bell at Belford in Northumberland. Then we had two nights at The Berkeley in London before returning to Malta to honour the terms of my leave. Alastair Bruce, one of the officers in *Sentinel*, and his girlfriend Myfanwy Phillips greeted us at the airport where I had arranged a surprise for Sue: a car of our very own! It was a fairly old Fiat Topalina but we were both proud owners and it was to give us sterling service. I drove my wife to our new home – a bungalow on a cart track leading nowhere which for some reason glorified in the wonderful name of Pope Alexander the Seventh Junction. Captain Van der Byl, the Commanding Officer of *Forth*, had generously given me seven days local leave. It was a time of perfect happiness, during which Sue and I started to get to know each other again. We had got married on the princely sum of thirteen shillings per day plus eight shillings married allowance. We had a house and a car we could call our own, and above all else we were together again. We were as happy as sand boys.

Our wedding.

Our honeymoon was sadly interrupted as I was recalled to *Forth* after only five days. The Captain said he was sorry but we were sailing in two days for Suez and he needed me back in the Wardroom as Mess Secretary. I was informed that we were having an extra seventy officers (or equivalent) billeted on us in the form of war correspondents, Suez canal pilots and other experts and would I kindly see that we had enough gin on board? The problem was a serious one. I had to make a quick visit to Saccone and Speed, our suppliers in Valetta and the following day (a Sunday) a special plane load of gin was sent out to the island. That night I put a notice on the board advising of an increase in the price of gin from twopence to twopence halfpenny (old pence). There was nearly a riot.

We sailed on the Monday morning and I had to leave Sue in the care of some of my chums serving in submarines, who were not coming with us.

The passage from Malta to Suez took approximately three and a half days. The captain explained to the ship's company the situation in Suez both from the political and the operational standpoint and the company was rapidly worked up to a war routine. My job was to work with the Deputy Supply Officer and to liaise with the salvage fleet which would be assembled from all over the world to clear the canal of the shipping which had been sunk by Colonel Nasser in order to block it. In particular I was to board each salvage ship as she came into port and be responsible for supplying her with everything that she needed. On the passage there was some spare time and a few of the younger officers including myself organised a roulette table. There was a lot of hot money with war correspondents' allowances being freely spent and we took the opportunity to make a profit for the mess.

We rendezvoused with the rest of the task force off Suez and watched the bombardment followed by the invasion of Egypt by our paratroopers. When ordered we steamed into Port Said, the first British ship, and we had no resistance in taking over the port. Of course history will be able to put the Suez operations into a better context than those of us who had taken part. However, from our point of view it was difficult to regard it as anything other than a successful operation botched up: we had taken charge of the Canal and it was desperately frustrating that the politicians made a nonsense of it by not letting us finish the job. Not only were we unable to complete the take over of the entire Canal, we could not even complete the clearance of the salvage operation.

During the two months that we were in Suez I had several visitors. One of these was an Old Sedberghian, Tony Peart, who was part of the Marine Commando Force and appeared dripping mud and blood on my pristine quarterdeck one afternoon. I sent him below, suitably admonished, for a bath and then invited him to join me for dinner. Another O.S., Tim Hoult, was a sub lieutenant in *Manxman,* a fast mine layer that did the 'potato run', bringing fresh supplies from Cyprus to Suez for the task force, which came alongside *Forth.* We would dine with each other in our respective ships whenever possible.

My job of looking after the salvage fleet was never dull. I can remember being particularly intrigued by two enormous German salvage vessels which were virtually self-sufficient as far as food and stores were concerned. They were able to last independently for periods of up to one year without requiring fresh supplies, although I was able to let them have some things they did not possess, such as milk and fresh vegetables.

Eventually it became clear that our presence in Port Said was no longer tenable and on 22nd December we turned tail and began the journey back to Malta. En route we ran into a Force Seven westerly, which considerably delayed our progress. It meant that on the 25th we were still at sea, and we reconciled ourselves to having a full-blown Christmas Mess Dinner as *Forth* battled her way forward through the adverse weather. Luckily she was reasonably stable, and it was possible for a Mess Dinner to be served with all the relevant glass, silver and china without being subject to more than an occasional minor incident. This was not the fate, however, of a mine sweeper whom we had passed at sea that day. I happened to be on the bridge just as we signalled "Happy Christmas". Back came the reply, "Happy Christmas be blowed – the bloody turkey's just fallen out of the oven!"

We arrived back in Malta on Boxing Day afternoon. I found to my chagrin that I was on duty and was not able to go home to my wife. I did manage, however, to arrange for her to join me on board for dinner in a private cabin. Thanks to one of my fellow officers who took over my duty, Sue and I were able to go home at around midnight and resume our delayed Christmas leave together. We were also able to pick up the threads of our aborted honeymoon, and start, once more, to get to know one another properly.

A short while into the New Year I was sent to the Royal Naval Air Station at Halfar on the south east corner of the island, to assist with the preparation of the prosecution case of the court-martial of an officer. My task was to carry out an accounting investigation and prepare a technical brief for the prosecutor. It so happened that I was to remain at RNAS Halfar for the rest of my time in Malta except for two weeks during the summer when I returned to *Sentinel* for the Summer cruise. Whilst there I spent some time as the Cash Officer, which meant having to handle the numerous different Mediterranean currencies with pilots coming and going the whole time. Luckily I had a very good petty officer writer or I would probably have been court martialled myself for mixing up the currencies.

During this time the National Service doctor at Halfar Rob Morley and I played golf at the Marsa Club against the CO and First Lieutenant of *Sea Devil*, a submarine in refit, Nigel Gilbert and Ian Morrison. This was only possible by getting our weekly four ball posted as a Sports Event in Malta's weekly orders under *Golf*: RNAS Halfar v HMS Sea Devil. My boss was then happy to let me have the afternoon off.

When we got into summer routine we worked at Halfar from 6.00 am to 1.00 pm followed normally by lunch in the ward room. This became very much a habit which stayed with me for the rest of my life and I have always worked a very long morning, usually starting at about 7.00 am. Sue would later claim somewhat ruefully that this didn't seem to stop me from working late in the office until about 7.00 in the evening.

Halfar was memorable in several respects,. There was a marvellous beach which was a popular lunch time and afternoon venue. During my time there our faithful little Fiat had a face lift from a friendly ERA who gave it a respray at the workshop. A rather less friendly fellow officer took me for a flight in his Meteor with (I am convinced) the sole object of making me violently ill ... but I managed to survive.

In the Spring of 1957 when Jol Waterfield, a submariner, left the island, we moved from Pope Alexander the Seventh Junction to his more traditional flat in Balzan, near the Governor's Palace. The building boasted a roof with quite a good view which made an excellent place for parties in the summer. The roof was reached by a narrow spiral staircase. When giving a dinner party we hoisted the dining table by ropes up the side of the house! We were now enjoying the splendid social life of Malta in what were effectively the last days of the Raj. We managed to live life to the full and all in all had a grand time. Many Saturday evenings we would go to the Marsa Club with various friends for a dinner dance which cost under a pound for the two of us. Most weeks there were cocktail parties and balls and dinners. That spring our parents visited us and we took great pleasure in showing them around Malta which not only has a fascinating history but was also particularly beautiful at that time of year. Sue's sister Jane came out to stay for a fairly lengthy trip and we introduced her to Roger Venables, a young submariner whom she was to marry some years later.

Ken Frewer, First Lieutenant of *Sentinel*, and his wife Jilly accompanied Sue and I on two camping trips to the neighbouring island of Gozo, where I was introduced to the joys of underwater fishing for one's breakfast. Chris Belton joined us on one of these trips with a girlfriend. Also in the Spring I took part in a memorable escape and evasion exercise, which involved walking the length of Malta without being detected by what seemed to be the entire population of the island who were engaged in attempting to ambush me. Needless to say I ended up in prison. April 21st was a memorable day: not only was it my 25th birthday but our combined pay and marriage allowance was more than doubled and I suddenly became much better off. I was invited to join *Sentinel* for the summer cruise again that year. We finished up in Venice and that was a memorable experience. I remember the pride with which I was allowed to take the con of *Sentinel* as we steamed up the Adriatic on the surface.

I took part in the round the island whaler race which happened every year. We had completed well over three quarters of the course when a sudden squall caused us to capsize. We were rescued by a tug and taken in tow, and gratefully accepted warm blankets and the head of the tug's engine room to restore ourselves. Unfortunately in the darkness the tow parted and our whaler was wrecked on the coast. I had some explaining to do to my Commanding Officer.

Late July found us planning to go home as my terminal leave was about to start. Then we were going to spend August driving home in our little baby Fiat to Newcastle. Richard Emden, who was Staff Officer Operations in Malta, was also planning to drive home and he arranged for both of our cars to have a lift on a tank landing craft to Sicily thus saving us quite a substantial cost of a ferry. Richard and Zannah were enjoyable companions and they needed their sense of humour as we camped our first night in Sicily. It didn't take long for our little Fiat to break down and there were various unintelligible conversations with a local garage proprietor during which the only word I could understand was "kaput"!!! Eventually, however, it was fixed and we continued on our merry way. We crossed the Messina Straits and camped in a beautiful meadow in south west Italy near the coast. As we were cooking our evening meal around our camp fire we became conscious that we were not alone and we were startled to find several men surrounding us. They explained that they had been sent by the Padrone to see whether we were all right and whether we needed anything apart from protection. As we assured them that we were quite self-sufficient my hand was straying to a large spanner which I kept handy in the car. However, the men disappeared without incident. Perhaps they had just been hungry!

Shortly afterwards we left the others to "go to Naples and Die" – and arranged to meet in seven days time at Harry's Bar in Venice. We went to Rome and got a much needed service for the car, and then set off to camp over the Apennines to visit Florence, en route to Venice. We did, in fact, meet the others on a canal boat very close to Harry's Bar on the seventh day and the four of us had a rollicking party in Venice. We then said goodbye and Sue and I travelled north over the Brenner Pass in pouring rain. That night we decided we could not face camping, so we stopped at the first pub we came to on the Austrian side of the pass, where the car spent the night in a pig sty and we were given the Honeymoon Suite! We had a lovely evening at the pub with a wonderful meal and a warm welcome from the locals who were great singers. We had an even better breakfast the next day and the whole bill was under a pound. The next night we valiantly attempted to camp again but were flooded out. We were very glad to get to Geneva the following day where we stayed with friends and slept in a real bed. We camped again in the forest at Fontainebleu. By now the Fiat was proving extremely difficult to start in the mornings. We got in the habit of leaving it parked on a hillside so that gravity could help first thing and save me a lot of elbow grease. Eventually we were to reach Newcastle where, once home, the Fiat promptly collapsed. We were able to get it going again only after a major overhaul.

4

In Practice as a
Chartered Accountant

He hath awakened from the dream of life.
Shelley

HEN WE ARRIVED BACK from Malta we stayed with Sue's parents. Having recovered from the marathon journey home our first task was to get Number Three Rectory Terrace fit for habitation. We had very little money and frequented furniture sales where we managed to buy all the essentials for less than £100 – no credit cards in those days! Interesting, too, to recall that 'essentials' at that time did not include fridge or washing machine and we began life at Rectory Terrace without either. Enthusiastically I turned myself into an amateur joiner and built some fitted wardrobes and we did most of our own decorating.

One luxury I was determined to have was a garage. A cheap option was to purchase a do-it-yourself affair which came in kit form. Having acquired the services of a builder to lay some concrete I rallied the troops to my aid: John and Malcolm, Brian Gillespie and his brother Neil all agreed to give up some spare time and assist in the construction of this architectural masterpiece. I thought we might as well make a day of it and bought in a barrel of beer, and Sue made lunch for us all. All went swimmingly and we were making good progress, with the sides in place and the roof ready to go on. We were in good spirits and were nearing completion when my father arrived. Neil happened to be holding up an overhead piece of the kit, but turned to speak to my father and in doing so let go of the piece he was holding. He had not realised, however, that the item was the critical support. Just as he stepped out of the way the precariously balanced construction veered alarmingly to one side and, almost in slow motion, each carefully placed piece fell gracefully in sequence, until the entire garage was no more than a muddled pile of kit pieces on the ground. Luckily we all saw the funny side of it. The barrel of beer came into its own and, suitably fortified, we started the whole process again from scratch. I was, at last, the proud owner of house and garage.

We moved in and I started to work at Graham and Spoor. Life soon took on a comfortable routine. The train ran at the bottom of the garden and the station was, conveniently, next door. Commuting to work was thus very straightforward and quick, and on most days in the early days I would come home for lunch. I remember on a Friday afternoon or evening buying chocolates as a weekend treat from a kiosk on the station bridge. Our family also extended quite soon with the acquisition of our first dog – a border terrier called Joker. That winter brought heavy snow: a real novelty for us all as we obviously had not had snow in Malta. Joker was a small puppy and loved the snow, bounding through the deep drifts up to his neck and barking wildly, much to our amusement.

I had formally joined Graham and Spoor as a qualified Senior on the first of October 1957 and from that time I started to learn how to be an accountant in practice. Looking back, I realise that I was to go on learning for the rest of my life. The partners of the firm were Percy Cooper and David Henson and my father and the three of them were busy building up a strong client base. It was not long before I started acquiring contacts of my own and gradually we began to attract the attention of bank managers, lawyers and stockbrokers as well as a colourful array of clients. One day a very pretty girl walked into my office, accompanied by three young children. Her story was a complicated one. She had married an Irishman who worked as a navvy on the roads earning a lot of money. Unfortunately, in his younger days he had been prevailed upon to complete a tax return fraudulently, claiming for a wife that did not exist and, each year, a new imaginary child. This girl had married him some years previously and was shortly expecting their fourth child and now thought it was about time to come clean. I had a very interesting meeting with the Inspector of Taxes but we subsequently got her husband off the hook without being sent to prison.

Professionally, those were exciting times. I joined the Union Club where I would meet friends and colleagues over lunch. We were young and enthusiastic and it seemed that the world was our oyster. On 1st January 1958 I became a Partner. We merged two smaller firms (Kingsley Allan and Watson & Pickering) where the firm's principal retired after a few months. In 1963 Malcolm brought his practice, John A Walbank, to merge with us, his Senior Partner having died the year before. Then in 1966 John Pashley and Ken Patterson (who had been articled in Graham & Spoor) brought in their firm, Joy Price. We were now growing quite fast and also establishing some useful connections. Each year we would take a party to The Northern Society of Chartered Accountants' annual dinner, and we would be invited as guests to the Law Society Dinner, all white tie affairs in those days. I started becoming involved with the Northern Society of Chartered Accountants more actively and regularly attended a weekend training course at Otterburn, a move which led indirectly to our merger with Joy Price. There was a good spirit in the office and we took on extra space in Norham House on the fourth floor. We were now getting busy and I was thoroughly enjoying myself. A busy professional life can be a lot of fun, and it was helped by the fact that many of our clients were also good friends. On our lists were some medium-sized companies with lots of problems and I always enjoyed the challenge that such cases offered. I began to take a particular interest in the problem of Share Valuations, although I had a growing bank of clients and I was, in effect, a General Practitioner.

On my return from Malta I had taken up again with Tyne Division RNVR and started going along once more to *HMS Calliope* on Monday nights. The difference was that I was now an Officer – a Sub Lieutenant. Sue was very understanding. She fully appreciated that Monday nights were sacrosanct and, in her words, on a Monday she accepted that I was married to Her Majesty the Queen. I also did occasional Wednesdays and weekends and every year would spend 14 days sea training in *HMS Northumbria* or in the Fleet. My routine on a Monday was to leave the office at around 18.00 and drive to *Calliope* where there would be tea in the wardroom. Divisions were at 19.00, evening quarters at 21.00. Afterwards we would have a drink in the wardroom before supper. After supper the port would be passed and it would often be quite late before I got home. There was a healthy social element to the Division, with frequent parties and formal dinners such as the Trafalgar and Samoa Dinners and the Summer Ball. I duly took my turn to propose the toast at the Samoa Dinner and was extremely lucky to discover John Masefield's epic poem on the subject for the occasion. It was all tremendous fun and a relaxing change from accountancy. I devoted a lot of time to *Calliope*, all of it, I think, well spent.

In 1959 I was promoted to Lieutenant, and the Captain of the Division, Douglas Thorburn, asked me to become Captain's Secretary. This position provided me with a fascinating insight into the workings of a Division and it was during this time that I established a great rapport with a character called Monty Norton. Although a civilian, Monty was employed by the Admiralty to run the Division from an administrative point of view. We had many adventures in our Minesweeper *HMS Northumbria*, some rather more hair-raising than others. Perhaps the most infamous was when we went aground at Holy Island. I can also remember an occasion in Portsmouth when my chum Derek Collings was driving and his orders were not transmitted properly to the engine room. Instead of going astern we went full ahead and rebounded with some force off the jetty of *HMS Dolphin*. I also established a good relationship with 6th Battalion Royal Northumberland Fusiliers (TA) through Frank Potts, with whom I played rugby in the second row for Northern.

I used to take some sailors to take part in combined exercises with the Sixth RNF. On one unforgettable occasion this involved a major battle on Holy Island with most of the TA Regiments in Northumberland taking part. Tyne Division covered itself in glory, landing marines through smoke and being well reported in The Sunday Times. I had infiltrated some junior officers on to Holy Island in mufti as spies and one New Zealand Sub Lieutenant disabled the field guns of 272nd Field Regiment TA by purloining their gun sights. The expression on the face of their Colonel when they were handed back to him at the washup outside the pub on the Sunday morning was a joy to behold! We also started to take parties of officers and ratings regularly to the Cairngorms on skiing trips. This tradition, once established, went on for a number of years, and one year we managed to persuade the Royal Navy to hold the Naval Ski Championship in the Cairngorms. Despite skiing conditions which were far from ideal it was a great success.

Calliope thus provided an excellent social life, and satisfied to a large extent my desire to remain within the Naval family. She also served another purpose, for I soon found that my association with her and with the officers enhanced my professional life, as there was a certain amount of 'cross-pollenation'. One overlap was Ken Patterson who, as previously mentioned, was articled to Graham Spoor and became a partner through the Joy Price merger in 1966. Ken was an officer on *Calliope*. Malcolm's wife Lalage also happened to be a WRNR Officer. John Mitcalfe, who became Captain of the Division, was a Director of a company who asked me to be their accountant and Alan Wilkinson, who also became Captain of the Division, was a Director of another client company. One evening as I was driving to *Calliope* over Benwell Hill I saw the silhouette of *Sentinel* glinting in the evening sunlight. She was obviously in the breaker's yard which was on the south bank of the river, opposite *Calliope*. I decided that I would take the opportunity to have a last look, and that night after supper a few of us rowed over to *Sentinel* and boarded her. It was rather depressing, but we helped ourselves to a few mementoes whilst we were there!

Our neighbours in Rectory Terrace, the Wright family, were particular friends and Captain Wright was a Merchant Navy Captain. His son John was keen on matters naval and one Monday evening I offered to take him down to *Calliope*. John liked what he saw and as a result enrolled in the Engine Room branch. After he had been commissioned in *Calliope* he asked to be transferred to the Royal Navy and is now an Engineer Captain RN. Somehow I feel slightly responsible!

Whilst in Malta we had made many friends among the First Submarine Squadron and now, in the late fifties, many of them had become Commanding Officers, having passed their "perisher". Newcastle was a popular run ashore for the sailors and so many submarines visited the River Tyne that Sue and I were able to renew these friendships. One evening we received a telephone call from Terry Thompson, who had been the navigator in *Sentinel*. He was calling from York to say that he had brought his midget submarine all the way north from Portsmouth via innumerable canals. There did not, however, appear to be sufficient water between York and Newcastle and he proposed to catch a train to see us. We met him about 10.30 that evening and I think we were up most of the night reminiscing.

As well as rejoining *Calliope* I also returned to rugger at Northern, where I competed for a place in the first team. Although I was still only 25 when I returned from Malta I had to train exceptionally hard to get fit. A year or so later Bobby Robinson, who was then President, asked me to captain the second team which became known as The Wanderers. At the age of 30 I gravitated to The Gypsies – the old men's team – and I finally hung my boots up at the age of 33 having captained The Gypsies, and having played in eleven Northumberland cup finals at differing levels and never been on a losing side. I share this record I think with Brindle Montgomery and Lance Robson, having had the luck to play for Northern in some of its vintage years.

As well as participating eagerly in the game, I also helped out on the Club's administrative side, serving on the Committee for twenty one years. I was Honorary Treasurer for sixteen of those years, until I handed the job on to Malcolm.

We had a great deal of fun and I will always remember our visits to Edinburgh where Northern would play varying opposition on the morning of an international. The Northern Club steward, Sergeant Stobart, was a great character and a very loyal servant to the club. One weekend we took him to Edinburgh with us. Long after closing hours I found him, with the apparent blessing of the hotel manager, serving behind the bar at the North British Hotel in Princes Street which happened to be where

Northern Wanderers, *circa* 1959. R.C.S. bottom row, fourth from right.

the England team were staying. The following day the bus returned to Northumberland and Sergeant Stobart continued to enjoy himself thoroughly when we stopped for lunch at Peebles. When the bus finally stopped at Bobby Robinson's for ham and eggs at midnight Sergeant Stobart was quietly put to bed. He returned home on the Tuesday and I do not believe Mrs Stobart let him out of her sight again.

On another occasion the bus stopped at the White Swan at Alnwick for us to refresh ourselves. An extremely jovial character was playing the piano and a great sing song developed. Every round of drinks included one for the pianist and by closing time the effect of alcohol and his exertions on the piano had reduced him to slumber. Someone had established that he lived in Dunbar so it seemed natural for us to put him on the bus since it was on our way to Edinburgh. When we eventually found his home, his mother expressed some astonishment informing us that her son was on his honeymoon in Alnwick!

One of the more amusing sidelines was an annual golf outing, generally to Hexham where among other trophies we played for the Hemming Award. In order to qualify one had to be still standing on one's feet at the end of the day and the award was then presented to the man who, in the opinion of the other members still standing, was considered to have 'enjoyed himself most' during the course of the day. In the old days the ceremony was carried out on the pavement of the Haymarket after the bus had decamped all the competitors.

Northern possessed three squash courts and, like many of the other playing members, I availed myself of the opportunity to play squash, a game which has the advantage of being relatively short and therefore suitable to fit in during a busy working day. At the age of 35, however, I took the decision to pack up squash as well as rugger. I had known one or two acquaintances who had had heart attacks or coronaries from such active exercise after that age, unless it was kept up regularly and thought it wise to concentrate on less physically taxing pastimes.

At around the age of 27 I started to play golf reasonably seriously. I had joined Northumberland Golf Club when I was a student, having learnt the rudiments of the game when I was 15. Now I started to play regularly with a handicap of eighteen. Northumberland Golf Club was an institution which could quite easily have been described by P. G. Wodehouse. On a Sunday morning there was a specific drill. The first four ball went off about 8.40am and was called the Dawn Patrol, followed at decent intervals by the Wreckers, the Senior Dentists and the Junior Dentists. My first golf had been played with the Senior Dentists because my father-in-law (who had been a junior county champion in days gone by) still liked a quiet Sunday morning round and the Senior Dentists were very generous with their putts to one another. I played with Nigel Ward, Gordon McKeag and Richard Mullens among others and we normally set off at about 9.20am on a Sunday morning, sometimes after early Church. Occasionally I would play with Sue in the evening in a mixed foursome. On these occasions we would follow the game with a supper of ham and eggs in the clubhouse – always excellent value. As a sportsman I continued to have reasonably good co-ordination and as my handicap began to decrease I started to win some medals and other cups. I found that it was wonderful relaxation from the office to go to the golf course for an hour or so and in those days of course the traffic was a lot easier, making it an altogether pleasant way to pass the time.

Sue and I had been married in Jesmond Parish Church. However, now that we had settled in Rectory Terrace we began to attend St Nicholas' Church, the old parish church of Gosforth which was just across the road. We have made it our own church ever since. It is an extremely old building, dating from 1170 but built on Saxon foundations and probably going back over a thousand years. In those days it was supposed that most of Newcastle was included in the parish of Gosforth. We have remained loyal to this church and all of our family christenings and weddings have been celebrated in St Nicholas. I also followed in my father's footsteps as auditor to the church.

Soon after my return to England from Malta I took up fishing. My father-in-law was a mad keen fisherman and in fact in his younger days he had fished for England in the annual match at Loch Leven. He took me to a beautiful place in Northumberland called Colt Crag which, although a reservoir, is mostly natural, and there he taught me how to fish: the art of casting, when to use different flies, and how to get the best out of a fishing boat. After he died I inherited his rods. A bit later Derek Knowles, who had become a chum through shooting, taught me how to fish the dry fly and to stalk trout (and later salmon). He had the shooting and fishing rights at Kidlandlee in the Cheviot foothills. There were wonderful mountain streams in which to practise the art of stalking and upstream dry fly fishing. Later still, Johnny Baxter taught me how to cast with a big rod. I will always be grateful to my mentors for having instilled a basic understanding of fishing into me. Fishing is now in my blood and is something I will enjoy and continue to learn until the day I die. Even then I am sure that I shall have covered only a tiny fraction of this wonderful sport.

On 9th January 1959 an event occurred which meant that our lives were never to be quite the same again. Our first child, Nicola, was born in a nursing home, during a snowstorm – a healthy seven and a half pounds. This great event was followed only fifteen months later by the arrival of Mark who was born at home on 7 April 1960. We were very grateful to have Nurse Armstrong living with us at Rectory Terrace for a week or so at the time. I remember coming back from a Mess dinner one night to find the house full of doctors drinking my whisky. They had been called because it was felt that Sue was ready to start her labour but having examined her they said they didn't think anything was likely to happen very soon. We all retired for the night and I went to my quarters which had been temporarily moved to the very top of the house. After what seemed to be five minutes Nurse Armstrong banged on my door and told me to come down and I found the doctor and gynaecologist back again and learnt that my son had been born. We now started living in a world of cots and prams and nappies, although of course in those days husbands were not expected to help as they are today and my involvement in the basic necessities of young children were relatively limited. However, with two very young children my wife did need some help in the house and over a period of about four years we had a succession of three wonderful au pair girls who provided an enormous amount of support. Two (Dagmar and Barbara) were from Germany, and then came Kiki, from Denmark. Nicola and Mark both went to nursery school and when she was five Nicola started at Westfield Junior School. Mark started at Newlands Prep School before transferring to NPS at the age of eight. With two young children around, the house took on a much more boisterous atmosphere. The two of them would play in the back garden when it was fine and at weekends we would take them for picnics to the coast. Wintertime meant sledging and traditional family Christmases and for those next few hectic years the house became cheerful and noisy and full of fun.

In the Summer of 1959 Sue and I took Nicola – then only a few months old – on holiday. We joined Malcolm and Lalage and their son Simon in North Cornwall. The holiday was a great success, we all fell in love with the place and thus began a tradition which has continued ever since. In those early days, when the children were growing up, we used to leave Newcastle on a Friday evening after I had left the office, packing the car and setting off at about 6.30pm with the children perched on top of the luggage. The aim was that they should sleep on the long journey south, but they were always far too excited and wide awake, certainly for the initial stages of the journey. We would stop for a picnic supper in the Dukeries at which point the children would be fully alert and chattering nineteen to the dozen. Then at around 2.00 am we would pull in for a later supper stop at Bath, by which time we would find two flushed and tousled heads nestled on the pillow, the slow regular breathing assuring us that the pair of them had at last fallen fast asleep. In those days of winding 'A' roads and not a motorway in sight the journey would take us 13 hours. Today we can do it in six and a half – although admittedly today's cars are designed to go much faster.

We took the doctor's house, Lees Nook, at Constantine Bay. It was an old Cornish smugglers' cottage which slept eleven. The garden was sheltered by a tamarisk hedge and opened straight on to the sand dunes – an ideal holiday spot for young children. An attraction for me was a splendid golf course in Trevose, nearby, and the fortnight's holiday would always pass by so quickly, with surfing and golfing being the two main activities and the children spending hours on the beach and swimming in the sea. Whilst the children were still very small we would go back to Constantine Bay every year in June; once they had started school we were confined to school holidays but still returned year after year, usually in August. It was in Cornwall that both of the children learnt the rudiments of golf, and they both took to surfing like ducks to water.

In those idyllic days when the children were young we would spend as much time as we could on trips with them. Closer to home we had invested in a tent and we would take them camping on the dunes south of Alnmouth or occasionally go across to the Lakes. Even though the North Sea is extremely cold, camping on the north east coast has a lot to recommend it.

Friends would often accompany us on these trips. I recall one incident in particular when Crispin Sadler and Mark got into trouble starting a fire on the dunes which required quick action by Malcolm and I to put it out.

I have never been particularly interested in motor cars or enjoyed driving – just as long as they do the job and get you from A to B. In 1959 we swapped the Fiat for an Austin A40. By 1961 we must have been doing well as I bought a new baby Fiat for Sue and we became a two car family! The A40 was replaced by a Triumph Estate car, one of several which we had. I have noticed that as vehicles have improved over the years the problems of cars not starting seem to have largely disappeared, although my cars do seem to have their fair share of troubles, probably because I am so unmechanical.

In 1959 I was asked by the Honourable Lady Waller to take on the post of Honorary Treasurer of Murray House Community and Youth Club. This was my first charitable job and I remained Treasurer for 13 years, after which I became the Chairman for four years. Shortly after I had joined, Peg Waller handed over the Chairmanship to George Bainbridge who became a firm friend. Murray House was situated just off Westgate Road, one of the more notoriously difficult areas of Newcastle. It had been established originally by the Admiralty Social Service Association after the First World War, when the Admiralty had cut back so savagely on their shipbuilding programme and had clearly felt a twinge of conscience about the number of ship yard workers thrown out of work. The Warden of the place was a character called Bill Gresham, who was subsequently appointed an MBE. Bill was a saint. He was not physically strong but he managed to keep control of Murray House in very difficult and challenging circumstances and was generally highly respected by the local community. A Gosforth based committee had made all the decisions about the running of Murray House. As times moved on I felt that that was wrong and that the West End of Newcastle should not be patronised in this way. When I became Chairman I therefore tried to involve the local community in running Murray House which by then had moved into a brand new building, after George Bainbridge and I had mounted a very successful appeal. However, it was very, very difficult to get the local people to take the responsibility and eventually the council had to take up the mantle.

Officers of HMS Calliope, 1970. R.C.S. bottom row, fifth from left.

Our life in Rectory Terrace had settled into a very comfortable and enjoyable routine. We sustained an active but simple social life, enjoying the company of friends at home. The children would be in bed early, and a favourite way to spend an evening would be to invite up to sixteen people in for a progressive bridge party, which would include a simple supper and beer or wine to drink. Talking of beer reminds me of my prowess as a home brewer. I had tried and failed to make wine, but then had a go at a very interesting home brew, which turned out looking and tasting just like the real thing. For our farewell party, we decided to invite all of the locals from the Terrace to come in and sample this delicacy, which they did with enthusiasm. The brew must have been much stronger than they – or I – suspected and a sight I shall never forget is that of the neighbours staggering home late that evening, many having to be helped along the way.

Through my links with *Calliope* and also through my professional life our social circle was really quite broad. Many of our friends lived in Northumberland or Durham and in summer particularly we would spend quite a lot of time with them in the country. For some time we considered moving out of the city ourselves, but in the end were persuaded to stay put for several reasons, convenient proximity to the office being one, and proximity to children's schools and both sets of grandparents being another. Also it meant that one was close to the Rugger club and the golf club. Sue, too, had an increasingly active social life. She didn't work while the children were young but was kept busy with coffee mornings and lunch parties with other young mothers who would meet together with all the children in prams and carrycots. She also became a member of the Newcastle and District Beagles and would go off enjoying herself beagling whilst I took my turn holding the fort with the children.

Graham and Spoor was still growing with more clients joining all the time. In 1968 Percy Cooper's son John joined the partnership. With John on board we reorganised the office once again and, now having taken over the whole of the fourth floor, we became more proactive, marketing the firm using our contacts amongst the major banks and lawyers. The Club network was one of considerable professional significance, and my circuit now included not only the Northern Counties Club but also (briefly) the Conservative Club. I was spending more and more time on trips to London, where I also became a member of the RNVR Club and the Army and Navy Club. I realised that I was becoming more ambitious about the future of the firm. We started to look at a merger with one of the big eight to give us better technical backup and a broader client base. Ken Patterson was approached by Gordon Howe, a partner in Arthur

Young McClelland Moore & Co. I took advice from Bill Mackey with whom I had played rugger and who had been my Assistant Treasurer at Northern. One morning early in 1969 Percy and I set off for London to meet with Gordon Howe and Derek Foster, two of the partners in AYMM. After many more visits and meetings with the firm's partners in London and Glasgow a merger was agreed in late 1969, to come into effect from April 1970. We started attending monthly partners' meetings in London. The Newcastle office was even busier than ever, and things augured very well indeed for the future.

In 1967 I was promoted to Lieutenant Commander in *Calliope*. It was at this time that we came ashore to new headquarters in Gateshead, although we still had our tender *HMS Northumbria* alongside. I started taking more responsibility and the following year John Mitcalfe, Commanding Officer, made me the First Lieutenant of the Tyne Division. My half-formed ambition of becoming Commanding Officer of the Division was now taking definite shape. No Supply Officer had ever before been made Commanding Officer but I could now see a path ahead for me to achieve this. I took my part-time parallel career seriously and worked hard at the job. I remember on one occasion John asking me to stand in for him at a formal visit by a Danish Cruiser to the River Tyne. Deciding that this was matter of duty I cancelled two appointments at very short notice and attended the event, which included a splendid thirteen course lunch. Of course as the senior British Naval Officer present I had to toast the Queen of Denmark and then had to keep up the pace as our glasses were constantly topped up with Carlsberg and schnapps for a succession of other toasts – thirteen in all! After lunch we were permitted a brief respite and a stroll around the upper decks before returning to find that the tables had been relaid with bottles of brandy!!

On a fourteen day sea training cruise when I was the Squadron Supply Officer we went through the Kiel Canal into the Baltic. I remember Raymond Allison and I getting into some trouble. I can also remember getting a very early bus from Helsinborg back to Landskrone after a terrific party on a glorious sunny morning. I was the only passenger when the bus started on its journey but by the time it arrived at Landskrone it had picked up at least 30 fellow travellers, all gorgeous young blonde girls!

With all this necessary intake of alcohol it is hardly surprising, I suppose, that the arrival of the breathalyser had a considerable impact on our lifestyle. As an exercise in PR – and in order to help ourselves to come to terms with this new device – we decided to invite the Gateshead Police to join us in the Division as our guests for supper one evening. After evening quarters none of us (quite uncharacteristically) drank very much.

At the end of the evening we all somewhat anxiously subjected ourselves to a breathalyser test – thankfully none of us needed to get a taxi home! The Division was growing in size at this time and consequently the administration was taking up more time. We had lost Monty Norton but gained a Staff Supply Officer as well as a Staff Officer. I got into the habit of having lunch in *Calliope* rather than in the Division each Tuesday with the Commanding Officer and the Staff Officer and one or two others, in order to catch up with the administration left over from the previous evening. By 1970 *Calliope* was a very significant part of my life. Sue was roped in on various occasions too, participating in the Summer Ball and occasional parties and visiting ships coming into the river. We started being regular invitees on such visits, not least, I suspect, because I was able to organize reciprocal hospitality in the Northumberland Golf Club.

The advent of the breathalyser was to affect another aspect of life in Newcastle at the time. In 1969 I had been made a Vice President of Northern Rugby Club which was now struggling to maintain its position as one of the leading rugby clubs in the north. Gosforth was becoming predominant in the north east whereas in contrast Percy Park, which pre-war and immediately post-war had been one of the leading clubs, had dropped back. The likes of Bobby Robinson and Andy Bell had been prime movers in the Club's success but I had played my last game of rugby in 1965 for Andy Bell's XV against Alnwick. Both Bobby and Andy were Northumberland farmers and, along with many of their kind, they were no longer prepared to travel every Saturday to Northern. It was thus that the breathalyser led to the rebirth of Alnwick. Northern would never be quite the same again. There were also so many other attractions for young men with new sports, better transport, and, perhaps above all, ladies who refused to accept the lore of the male rugby club.

My golf was fitfully improving and I started playing more widely. I joined Foxton Hall Golf Club at Alnmouth and I also played at Bamburgh. I enjoyed golf outings with the Northern Society of Chartered Accountants versus the Lawyers and the Inspectors of Taxes and matches at Brancepeth and Hexham particularly stick in my mind. Perhaps my finest hour was when I reached the final of the Britten Cup at Northumberland against David Moffat, a former English International. I lulled myself into a false sense of security in that game by leading three up after 18 holes, enjoying a good lunch, only to be beaten narrowly at the end of the day. However, my handicap had come down to six and I felt confident that I could hold my own in any company.

As I played less rugger I started shooting. My father had taken up shooting late in life but had a gun in shoots at Harbottle and Felton and took me to both. I bought an AYA shot gun and had some lessons with my great friend Derek Knowles who had helped me to fish and was also prepared to give me a lot of friendly advice about shooting. Derek and I shot together at Kidlandlee and a bit on the Blagdon Estate. I also had an interest in a small shoot at Bedale in Yorkshire and went rough shooting with John and Malcolm at Lamesley. I joined Johnny Baxter's mini Hare-hope syndicate on Ted Wrangham's estate where there was a beautiful grouse moor. This was always a good family day out, as Judy Baxter would valiantly take charge of all the small children in a tent while the rest of us were either beating or shooting. Our wives were intrepid beaters and it was here that Mark started taking his turn in the beating line at the tender age of three years! The head keeper, Willie Smail, had quite a job keeping the beating line straight. I decided it was time I had my own gun dog and invested in a large and undisciplined but affectionate springer spaniel whom we called Punch.

The family were growing up all too quickly. Nicola moved from Junior to Senior Westfield although she was destined to go eventually to the Mount School at York. Mark was preparing to follow in the family tradition and take the Common Entrance to Sedbergh. We were lucky in that both sets of grandparents lived locally and were able to take an active role in their grandchildren's upbringing, although sadly in 1969 Sue's father died from emphysema, which had been gradually worsening. The proximity of our parents meant, too, that Sue and I were free to have some holidays alone, once in Portugal and on another occasion in Tunisia. In 1969 we paid a nostalgic visit to Malta, where we had started our married life. We found that there were few signs left of the Raj and Grand Harbour was occupied by the United States Navy. We met Anthony, Maureen and Judy Tapp and thoroughly enjoyed their company. Little did I then think that Anthony would figure quite largely in my life before very long.

We also managed an occasional weekend in the Lakes at Ullswater. On one occasion in 1969 we were joined by the Gillespies and the Tapps at Sharrow Bay. I must have been fit at that time because I ran *up* Pike-o-Stickle and back down again, passing the others on the way as they were coming up. On my return to base I had time to enjoy three pints in the Dungeon Ghyll pub before the others arrived back.

We had got into a habit of spending Easter with Sue's sister Jane who had married Roger Venables. One memorable Easter in 1969 in Ireland we joined them at Drenagh, the family home of the McAuslands where they lived for two years while Roger was driving a submarine out of Londonderry. I have happy recollections of Roger and I climbing a moun-tain and developing a thirst that required quenching with plentiful supplies of Guinness. On our return to Drenagh we were put to work decorating the spare bedroom. The wallpaper seemed to have a mind of its own and refused to lay vertically down the walls – we were not popular.

Shortly before Christmas in 1969 we moved house. Number 5, Graham Park Road in Gosforth had been the home of Winty and Rose Ellis, who were a sort of honorary aunt and uncle of mine. It was a much more substantial house than Rectory Terrace, and had a lovely, secluded walled garden. Just after moving in, we gatecrashed our next door neighbours' New Year Party. From then on the Norbury's were to become firm friends. The whole family was looking forward to the next chapter of life in Graham Park Road.

What of my life so far? I had played my part in building up the practice of Graham and Spoor and had been partly instrumental in the merger with the leading firm of Arthur Young. I had also pursued a parallel naval career with the clear prospect of becoming Captain of the Division. In sport I had left the violent sports of rugby, squash and skiing behind but I was proficient at and enjoying golf, fishing and shooting. I had the beginnings of a social conscience through my work for Murray House and the Church. And I was blessed with a wonderful happy family with the best wife in the world, two super children and a new home with a lovely garden. Life was full and satisfying and there seemed to be little more that one could wish for.

5

I Break My Back

Oh! Calamity!
Robertson Hare

 N AUGUST 1970 I was staying with John and Zan Baxter at their house in Alnmouth, together with Malcolm. Both the families had gone ahead to Cornwall and we planned to join them the following week. I remember playing golf at Foxton, where I was a member, on the Friday and meeting a lot of friends at the house where we were staying. However my memory of that Friday evening is not clear. We were going to shoot grouse the following day at Harehope Moor, not far away. I don't know exactly what happened but I must have walked in my sleep and somehow fallen over a balustrade into the central hall. I had clearly done myself some serious damage because although I could not feel any pain I could not move my legs to get up. An ambulance arrived and I was put on a stretcher. The pain started to hit me as I was moved. I was given morphia but as I was driven to Ashington along twisting country roads the pain grew steadily worse. By the time we arrived I think I was screaming and I can remember one of the nurses at Ashington hospital telling me to pipe down. I was not allowed any more morphia and the agony continued through the rest of that night and for most of the first day, which I spent on a bed which turned through 360°. My parents arrived and I put on a brave face but I didn't really want to talk. The Consultant Orthopaedic Surgeon examined me and tested my body with a pin for signs of feeling. I could not feel anything in my legs. He tried to reassure me that it was early days and that I would probably get some feeling back, although just how much was not yet clear. The following day Sue arrived from Cornwall. The family hols had been rudely interrupted and she had come at once when she heard the news, leaving behind the children who were really too young to grasp the reality of the situation. She was bravely cheerful and I can recall thinking how beautiful she looked.

Various friends also called to see me and my parents visited regularly every day. Unable to do anything further, practically, Sue returned to Cornwall to be with the children and I began to settle into a routine in the hospital. My bed would be turned twice a day to prevent bed sores, so I spent a certain amount of time lying on my tummy. My bladder would not work so I had an indwelling catheter. However blockages were frequent and a doctor would have to be called to free it and put in another catheter. Often I would have to endure long delays during which the pain of a swollen bladder became insupportable and in frustration I would swear at the nurses and anyone else who happened to be passing.

The pain in my back where my spinal cord had been fractured was wearing off and fortunately did not leave a lot of secondary pain. I have since discovered that this is not the case with many paraplegics who experience pain in areas where the nerves are trying to reach. Very slowly I started to get some feeling below the waist, which was just about where the fracture had occurred. I could feel the top part of my thighs and very gingerly started flexing my thigh muscles (quadriceps). Below the knee there was nothing. At the back of the thigh and around my buttocks there was nothing. The Consultant came every few days with his pin and said he was pleased with my progress.

I gave up smoking because it no longer appealed to me lying on my back. I never smoked a cigarette again although I became an occasional cigar smoker for a further ten years or so.

I had been at Ashington for two weeks when Jack Foster came to see me. Jack was an old friend who also happened to be a neurologist and he talked to me at length about the future. He told me that I would be permanently paralysed but that I might get enough movement to walk with sticks. However, without any feeling in the gluteus muscle (in the backside) I would be unable to balance. There would, he told me, be no more golf. Jack and I had played often together in the Park. Jack also warned me that my sexual function would be dodgy in the extreme, and might vary from nothing at all to a performance that would be something less than brilliant.

Before Jack's visit I had been living very much from moment to moment. After he had gone I think I wept for the first time as the full impact of the vast change in my life hit me. Golf had been a large part of my life. It seemed very unfair that I would no longer be able to enjoy it and I wondered whether I would be able to do anything at all in the way of sport. I also began to worry about Sue and me together with an inadequate love life. I often felt very depressed in those early days, thinking about being so long in bed and worrying about how I was going to travel to work and get around generally.

I remember one occasion which bucked me up. Sue brought the children and the dogs with her one day when they had all returned from Cornwall. The dogs were not allowed in the hospital but my bed was moved across to the window and I was able to look out at them playing on the grass. This small incident gave me an enormous amount of encouragement and also made me determined to think positively about the future.

A number of problems began to develop in my legs, largely because Ashington Hospital seemed to be very short of physiotherapists. I hardly received any treatment and as a result my legs became swollen and almost impossible to move. In fact lesions were building up and, although I did not realise it at the time, when I did move to a Spinal Unit they would have a major task in getting me going at all. It was Jack Foster's initiative that got me moved to Pinderfields, the Spinal Unit in Wakefield. He knew John Cook, the Consultant Neurologist in charge of the Unit very well, and made arrangements for me to go there five weeks after the accident. An ambulance was arranged and Sue came with me on the journey, which I recall as being extremely long and tedious. It was over 100 miles – a journey that Sue would have to make many times over the ensuing months.

6

Pinderfields Spinal Unit

What's amiss I'll strive to mend, and endure what can't be mended.
Isaac Watts

HE SPINAL UNIT at Pinderfields General Hospital, Wakefield, is deservedly renowned for its work with people who suffer serious spinal injuries and had (and still has) a reputation as the Stoke Mandeville of the North – although I do recall one ex-patient who referred to Stoke as "the Pinderfields of the South". It was known to all and sundry by the familiar title of "F1", the number of the ward. But F1 was more than just another ward in a hospital. It was very much a world within a world; a microcosm; something of a law unto itself. Ground rules that were typical in other hospitals were ignored. Everyone was encouraged to get up and get moving as quickly as possible, and by having the freedom of the hospital and its spacious grounds most patients could progress to a reasonable level of independence.

In September 1970 I arrived at Pinderfields by ambulance from Ashington, a very long and tedious journey. Sue came with me which was a great comfort, but my morale was not very good.

Perhaps it was because Jack Foster had briefed John Cook about me, perhaps it was because I was a professional man, a partner in a firm of Chartered Accountants, that I was given a room to myself, rather than being put in a ward. The room was a padded cell, left over from the days when the hospital had been a mental asylum. It was just big enough to take a bed and a small table for my odds and ends. It would be quite useful to shut myself off into my own private world on some occasions over the next few months.

By the time I got to Pinderfields, both my legs were very swollen and it was impossible for me on my own to bend them at the knees. This was due to the almost total lack of physiotherapy available at Ashington. There were no physiotherapists at Pinderfields but instead they had Remedial Gymnasts (RGs) and their college was in Wakefield. The leader of the team was Maurice Smart, later to be awarded the MBE, and I took to

51

him immediately and grew to respect and admire his devoted attention to his patients, his enormous patience and persistence to get them to achieve what he knew they could if they worked hard enough. His first task was to get my legs back into some reasonable shape. He took it gently, which was just as well because I could feel down the front of my thighs to the knees, which were agony because the cartilage and ligaments had all seized up. Gradually he brought more movement into the legs and each day I would be able to move them wider and bend the knees until at last I could bend them completely. He explained that I had been lucky in still having use of the quadriceps muscles in my thighs. I would have to work hard to build them up, but in due course they would provide the motive power which would enable me to walk forwards. At this stage I was still lying on my back but I could now, unaided, lift each leg without assistance and hold it in a position above my head.

The next stage was getting into a wheelchair. Maurice brought me one from the store and I gingerly tried to swing my legs over the side of the bed. With the aid of an RG I sat up for the first time – and nearly passed out! My balance had completely gone and I had to sit still for half an hour until I got used to an upright position. Funnily, my back did not hurt very much. It took two RGs to get me from the bed to the wheelchair – an operation which I would soon learn to do on my own as naturally as an able-bodied person. At this point I had very little muscle power in any of my limbs and Maurice gave me spring-loaded dumb bells to squeeze to exercise my wrist and forearm muscles.

The Charge Nurse at Pinderfields was John Mullins and he was a tower of strength, providing leadership and administration to the operations of the unit. The nurses were a superbly trained team of both sexes, and would generally be extremely strong which was just as well, as they had to lift all the patients several times a day. I was moved every few hours in bed so that I would not develop bed sores. (That this had not happened at Ashington was only due to my short stay there and the excellence of my skin tone, and I was lucky that I had not arrived at Pinderfields with bed sores. It was quite common for patients to arrive with bed sores because only at spinal injury units was there real knowledge and experience in handling paraplegics.)

Before long I met the most important person at Pinderfields in the life of a paraplegic – Mr Smith, the consultant urologist. In these days of high technology we tend to take for granted the ability to extrude polythene and manufacture all kinds of plastic products. However, not many years ago, the life expectancies of paraplegics was minimal because of the problems of chronic infection resulting from a paralysed bladder. These days, with plastic catheters emptying the bladder all the time it is possible for paraplegics to have a normal life expectancy, but in the first few months after a traumatic accident it is absolutely vital to ensure that the urinary system is operating satisfactorily. Complications arise to disturb a paraplegic's smooth working in life, in this area far more than in any other. I have described, in the previous chapter, my frustrations with blocked catheters at Ashington. This happened less frequently at Pinderfields because of the better realisation of urinary problems. Because of the danger of infection with an indwelling catheter it wasn't long before John Cook took me off catheters altogether and taught me his trick of how to empty my own bladder. This entailed sitting on a toilet, using a finger cot on the index finger and pressing (via the anal passage) on the prostate at the same time straining as hard as possible. Throughout the day and night I wore a sheath with a leg bag to avoid accidents (which still happened!) and there have been significant developments in the efficiency of this equipment over the last thirty years. Several times in my sojourn at Pinderfields I would visit Mr Smith who would test that my urinary system was operating by inserting coloured fluid and watching it flow through my kidneys and bladder on a television screen. Luckily I didn't have many complications, although most patients certainly did.

At the same time as emptying the bladder when straining and using John Cook's trick, the bowel would be emptied automatically. However, at Pinderfields, everyone's bowel (which was just as paralysed as the bladder) was evacuated manually each week by the nursing staff – an unpleasant task which was performed in bed with the patient having been given a suitable stimulant the night before. Difficult cases might require an enema! The bowel has remained a problem area for me in the last thirty years and I have learned that it pays to treat it with great respect and never leave anything to chance.

After I had got around the ward in my wheelchair and generally become acclimatised, Maurice Smart started on the next phase of my rehabilitation – to stand up and walk, leaning on parallel bars. Before this was possible it was necessary to fit my legs with steel calipers, to lock my ankles, which would otherwise turn over and do a lot of damage to the ligaments, and my knees because they were not yet strong enough to take the weight of my body without buckling. These calipers were monstrous affairs, seemed to weigh a ton and were difficult to put on. They were secured around the calf and thigh and were most uncomfortable. However, when I was thus equipped, I attempted to stand up. I placed my wheelchair at the end of the parallel bars and took a firm grip on the bars themselves. I got half way up and lost my nerve. Two RGs grabbed me and held me upright. The balance was very difficult to come to terms with and I think it was worse than anything that I have done since the accident, but gradually I got used to it and then I was able to swing myself along and I was, after a fashion, walking on a horizontal plane. This was the first of many tortuous sessions on the parallel bars during which I slowly regained my permanent balance and built up the strength in my upper body, without which nothing in this field is possible.

I had been at Pinderfields for a few days when I had my first visitor, Anthony Tapp (known to his friends as Soss) who lived at The Bridge House in Cattal, a small village near Wetherby and whose business, Tapp and Toothill, the printers, was situated between Leeds and Wakefield. We had met a year previously when on holiday in Malta and found ourselves staying, with our wives, at the same hotel. We had many things in common, one of which was that we had both been Sub-Lieutenants in the Royal Navy during our National Service. Soss arrived one day around 5.30pm, produced a bottle of sherry and for most of the rest of my time in Pinderfields came to see me about this time of day, every third day or so bringing another bottle. It may have been reasonably convenient for him, after work, but this great act of friendship and devotion gave me a huge amount of pleasure, gave me a point of time each day when I knew a bit of my past would become reality again and gave me huge hope for the future.

I slowly started moving around the ward, which had about thirty patients at any one time. I was an odd man out in various ways. I was not totally paralysed with a complete break of the spinal cord; mine was only partially broken and I might get back quite a lot of movement. Most patients had a complete break, meaning that they would never get any movement below the waist and several had a break higher up the back, towards the neck (a tetraplegic) meaning that they did not have full control (or power) over their arms and hands. I was well-educated, with a professional background and the apparent self-confidence to take in my stride the dreadful realities of what had happened to me. Not everyone could. Because I had been put in my own private room (cell) there was probably an initial view that I was rather stand-offish. If so, it was rapidly dispelled when I got around and talked to everyone else and we discussed each other's problems. Also working together in the gym and swimming pool brought all the patients together, sharing similar objectives and working towards a common goal. In another way I was in different circumstances. My job was essentially sedentary and it was clearly going to be possible for me to return to my practice and work at the desk in my office in a wheelchair and do most of what I had been able to do previously, before the accident. Many of the other patients were not so lucky. I can remember one man who had a flourishing business as a roofing contractor and broke his back falling from a half-built roof. His business went into liquidation, and he would never again be able to do the job for which he had been trained. In various ways I was able to help and give advice to some of my fellow patients, but always as a friend and not on any professional basis.

One day in early November I had an unexpected treat. Northumberland were playing Yorkshire at rugger at Headingly in Leeds and Fenwick Allison, Andy Bell and others arrived to collect me and take me to have lunch with the team and then to watch the game. John Cook was very happy to let me go and it was a memorable day – I had so much to drink that I can't remember the score, but I was with a lot of old friends and I was looked after most hospitably and taken back to the Unit in great form. To the best of my memory this was my first expedition out of hospital after my accident.

Sue made many visits to me while I was in Pinderfields, although it was a dreary drive of about 100 miles (200 return). I looked forward to these visits enormously, probably out of proportion because they brought back to me that I was a family man with responsibilities and whatever my problems were, the welfare of the whole family was top priority. Mostly Sue would come to see me at a weekend and when the time came that I could be taken out from the hospital, the Tapp family invited us to their home for Sunday lunch. This would involve Soss setting up a complicated arrangement of duckboards to get me and my wheelchair into the house, although later I would be able to walk in on crutches. The Tapp loo was a monument, mounted on three stairs at the back of the downstairs toilet and it was a major effort to seat me on this throne! I used to look forward very much to Sunday lunch with the Tapp family who were always so hospitable and helpful.

One of the most pleasant means of rehabilitation was swimming and once a week the Spinal Unit had unfettered use of the Pinderfield Baths. It was quite a long way from the Unit so it was a bit of an expedition on a wheelchair, which added to the enjoyment of the occasion. I found that the only satisfactory entry into the water would be to transfer from my wheelchair to the Baths' own wheelchair and get lowered down a ramp into the water. A feeling of freedom as you floated off the chair with apparently weightless limbs was sublime and we all made the most of it. But the RGs worked us hard because the real purpose was to re-build lost muscles and I had to do twenty lengths before being allowed to enjoy myself! We played a very amateur type of water polo, which was fun and was still utilising all the muscles.

Much time was spent in the gym and I sweated a lot trying to get myself fit. At first, it was all a question of mastering the balance of standing up on the parallel bars and improving one's arm muscles, lifting one's body on the bars in quite simple exercises. But later I got down to weight lifting, lying on a bench with successively larger weights being loaded on to me. I never achieved any great distinction but I certainly developed stronger muscles. The exciting game of wheelchair basketball was the most popular pastime in the gym and a great amount of energy was expended on it. I have rarely taken part in a more dangerous sport. No quarter was asked or given and crashes between chairs were normal, not unusual – obviously hands, arms and legs all suffered a great variety of injuries, mostly not serious although I can remember a broken arm. Being paraplegics we could feel little or nothing in our legs so there were few inhibitions in putting them at risk. By the time I left Pinderfields anyone with aspirations in disabled sport was training hard in the gym every day for the forth-coming battles that would take place between the different Spinal Units in the country, with the ultimate prize being a place in the British team in the Olympic Paraplegic Games.

I recall an Open Day when a great variety of sports was laid on. I rather fancied myself at table tennis, but I was resoundingly beaten by a woman who turned out to be the redoubtable Lady Masham – later to found and become President of the Spinal Injuries Association. She was a demon at table tennis and had a special table fitted in her home where she could practise on her own. Our paths were to cross in the future. Around this time I was fitted with shorter calipers because by now my knees had strengthened sufficiently for me to stand up. They fitted into the heel of an ordinary pair of shoes and had velcro fastenings below the knee. They were infinitely better than the larger calipers that I had had to wear up to now on the parallel bars, although they were still very heavy. I tried to play table tennis in them standing up but could not move quickly enough on my crutches and had to hold the bat in the same hand as one of the crutches, so I soon went back to playing in the wheelchair.

Ex-patients used to join us regularly for a free lunch and a spot of table tennis, archery, swimming or basketball using the hospital facilities and they performed a valuable function as a link with the outside world. Compared with the calm and quiet of most hospitals, F1 was often more like Clapham Junction. Wheelchairs whizzed around, with fairly athletic-looking men and women propelling them. Patients who were temporarily stranded in bed would be watching TV, listening to music or chatting to visitors (there were no formal visiting hours), while staff going off duty would be asked to call at the bookies, or the chippy, or the off-licence.

There was a kind of belligerent bravado about F1, as if, in spite of paralysis, one must be positive and this created a kind of solidarity between patients.

I met many interesting and fine people in F1 and particularly enjoyed the companionship of David Rogers who was a student, twenty years younger than me. We have kept in touch ever since.

John Cook and I had various discussions about many subjects as we got to know each other rather better, and he asked me if I would give the Consultants and Senior Doctors at the hospital a lecture on tax planning. I got some up-to-date information from my office and spent an enjoyable evening with these learned medical men who wanted to pay as little tax as possible (like most of us). I don't think I was able to help them a great deal as the opportunities for tax saving by employees are very limited, and most of them were employed full time by the NHS.

I came home for a weekend at the end of November. Sue made up a room for me in the dining room. It was wonderful to see the children who regarded me, or rather my wheelchair, with a great deal of curiosity. By the time Christmas came I had advanced sufficiently to walk upstairs and was able to sleep in my own bed for the first time and have a bath in my own bathroom. I was at home for Christmas and New Year and on Christmas morning we held open house after Church because it was obviously easier for me to stay at home in my wheelchair. Many friends came. We have had the same party on Christmas Day ever since.

Back in Pinderfields after New Year I did more intensive work on the parallel bars, getting my muscles to develop further and starting to walk longer distances on my new elbow crutches. I remember one day in the gym when I was resting, a rugby league player who had permission to train in the gym sat beside me. I could not help comparing his huge, well-proportioned leg muscles to my skinny ones. My leg muscles had been like his before my accident and I resolved to try and get my thighs closer to their previous shape.

Social life in the Spinal Unit was quite varied. One evening I was invited to take part in a darts match at a nearby pub. There was a unique difference between the way our hosts and we, the guests, played. They threw conventional darts to a conventional dart board. We used our bows and fired our arrows into special targets, made like a dartboard on a twenty-five yard range at the back of the pub. It sounds easy, but took a lot of practice to achieve proficiency. However, we all drank the same beer! Occasionally some of the nurses would help some of the more capable (well rehabilitated) patients to push themselves down to the nearest pub at lunchtime. It was about half a mile away and was (unusually) accessible for wheelchairs. On the way back a bit of a race developed, and I think some of the nurses were disciplined for leading their patients astray. Sue came down to visit me during January and I can remember Ben and Elke Smith arriving and taking me out for lunch one day. I was definitely getting a festive spirit.

As the time came for me to leave Pinderfields, Maurice Smart took a particular interest in making sure that I was as well-equipped as possible to lead a normal, useful life. I remember he told me that the leg bag which we used would hang better down the thigh if you cut off most of the connecting pipe. It would then be less likely to twist and there would be less chance of an accident – little things like that made such a practical difference to minimising the hassles of life as a disabled person. Because he knew that I planned to go upstairs to bed he took me to an adjacent staircase and taught me how to climb upstairs using one crutch and a banister. He also taught me the best way to get up a few steps when there was no handrail. Finally, he gave me some very good tips on exercising so that I could keep my body as fit as possible. I think that largely as a result of Maurice's advice I have managed to stay pretty fit for most of the nearly thirty years since I left Pinderfields.

I had a last discussion with John Cook before leaving and I asked him to give me some targets to aim at so that I might achieve some more recovery, although it was not expected that I should achieve anything very dramatic. I had in fact achieved quite a lot during the five months in Pinderfields and the most that I could expect beyond this would be getting used to coping better with my problems, developing short cuts and getting myself really fit. However, John suggested that I could, by exercising hard, get some more movement in my gluteus muscle (in the backside). This controls the balance when standing and it did give me a target to aim at. Unfortunately, although I worked at it for two or three years really quite hard my gluteus did not realise any further recovery.

I left Pinderfields on February 1st 1971 and returned to my office the following day. I saw no point in hanging around any longer and I had to get on with my life. Reflecting on my time at Pinderfields I was able to acknowledge that it had been a time of achievement, of hard work and quite a lot of fun. I retained – and still retain – considerable affection for Pinderfields and for the people that made it work.

7

Picking Up The Threads

No one knows what he can do until he tries.
Anon.

RETURNED HOME from Pinderfields with three main
ambitions. Firstly, I was determined to recover my quality of
life, as far as was humanly possible on my part. Resuming a
full family life ranked second, and, thirdly, I wanted to play
a full role once again as a partner in Arthur Young. I had some doubts
about what was possible and considerable uncertainty as to how much
more improvement in muscle power I would realise. But I was bolstered
by the encouragement of Maurice Smart, John Mullins and others from
Pinderfields and I determined to do my best.

I was very glad to get home; to live again with my family and have all
my old familiar things around me. We made some small alterations: a
hand grip here, a rail there, and an en suite bathroom in our bedroom
made life much easier. Sue and I were both relieved that we had completed
the move to Graham Park Road, because the doorways generally were of
generous proportion and my wheelchair fitted through them without
much trouble. Downstairs I used the chair which Pinderfields had given
me and bought another from the local wheelchair suppliers, Peacocks, to
use upstairs. I needed the upstairs chair to move from bed to toilet and
bath and of course to get my clothes from the wardrobes and drawers.
Our staircase was also generously proportioned and, as I had been taught
by Maurice Smart how to climb stairs leaving one crutch at the bottom
and making use of the other crutch and the banister rail, the stairs caused
me no great problem. The chair downstairs was essential whenever I
needed to pour my friends a gin and tonic. Able-bodied people take such
simple things for granted. However, if both hands are taken up with
crutches, even though it means being able to stand eyeball to eyeball with
somebody, it is impossible to handle a bottle and a glass as well. The
downstairs chair was also useful in enabling me to carry things around,
for example the post, from the front door to my desk in the study. A

simple task, but one which took some practice. Some things were more difficult to handle than others, and Sue was not best pleased when a bottle of wine slipped between my legs and spoiled the dining room carpet.

I returned to work the day after I came home from Pinderfields. I could not drive my car at first and Malcolm gave me a lift to the office for the first few weeks. Although I could walk into the office on my crutches, it was essential that another wheelchair be purchased for office use, giving me the ability to get around my own room and those of the other partners. I shall describe in more detail my return to Arthur Young and all that it entailed in a later chapter.

At this stage Sue was very involved with her catering business which really started in a small way when the children went to school. She wanted to combine a career which utilised her love of cooking with looking after the family. A demand for cooking at private functions led to her creating a reputation for good cooking and she built up a flourishing enterprise. This led to cookery demonstrations for housewives who wanted to learn how to make entertaining easier, and a natural evolution when I returned from hospital was the start of men's cooking classes on Monday evenings. I was no longer required to attend *Calliope* so Sue devised this method of occupying my time. The difference with the men's classes was that, having cooked the food, we then consumed it (and drank my wine). We had a passing out dinner at the end of term and the wives were invited both as guests and as judges of their husbands' efforts.

As well as cooking Sue made the men take their turn at washing up and on one occasion some surprise was expressed that the hands of an eminent concert pianist should be sullied by dishwater. On another occasion an enthusiastic interpretation of a simple instruction to grate a lemon resulted in its entire destruction, pith and all. Perhaps the most memorable occasion was when a doctor was preparing a boned stuffed chicken and feeling somewhat ill at ease with his efforts was seen extracting from his medical bag a surgical needle to better sew up the fowl.

It was necessary for any car that I was to drive to be fitted with hand controls. Although I could move my legs and bend my knees I did not have sufficient control to operate a clutch or brake pedal safely. I did teach myself, however, to work the accelerator pedal. So many modern vehicles are fitted with an automatic gear box that the clutch is no longer a problem, and the only hand control that I now have is on the foot brake. In those early days, however, soon after my accident, we spent quite a bit of time searching for the best hand controls and having the manual transmission on our existing cars adapted. I had to take a driving test and I can remember the courtesy which the examiner extended to me on that occasion. It was a wonderful feeling to be able to drive again and the wheels of my car were – and still are – for me, an extension of my legs.

My attention turned to taking exercise and getting myself really fit. I was allowed to use the University gym which was fully equipped with training weights and a lot of apparatus, though not much of it was a great deal of use to a paraplegic. I persevered with my weight training for several months but the thing which was of most benefit was walking around on my crutches. Gradually my muscles developed, and my shoulders became much stronger. I put on a lot of upper body weight and became almost pear-shaped. Although I did not realise it at the time, however, I was building up big problems for the future because the human body is not designed to take such pressure on the shoulders and eventually the ligaments and tendons were to wear out. At the time all I wanted was to be fit and strong – and that I became. I started taking part in a lot of outdoor activity.

In the summer of 1971, with the help of various friends – in particular Derek Knowles – I started fishing again. I found that once I was in a boat my legs were not really necessary, and with my new found upper body strength I could row a boat quite satisfactorily. From a secure position at the centre of the boat I could fish quite easily, because it is not necessary to cast a very long line when fishing from a drifting boat. The following year Derek, Sue and I went fishing in Ireland, to Currerevagh on the western shore of Lough Corrib and we were all initiated into the mysterious art of 'dapping' – trying to catch the wild brown trout that frequented that great lake. We had a great welcome from Harry and June Hodgson who ran the country house hotel in Currerevagh and they provided wonderful hospitality. The ghyllies would come round to the hotel each morning and Harry sent us out with old Martin Molloy who knew every inch of the lake but could no longer see where he was, relying on us to describe the features of the nearest island. He couldn't thread our mayflies onto the hook so we learned effectively how to do it all ourselves. He taught us how to count "God Save The King" before striking and we have used the art of dapping in Northumberland and Scotland on many occasions since.

I started shooting again in the winter of 1971, depending, at first, on my friends to drive me around in Land Rovers and put me down in a portable seat. Eventually I acquired my own Land Rover and, later still, Range Rovers, which were specially adapted. A paraplegic can shoot quite effectively from a solid seat, particularly one with some swivel and, with due supervision and practice, can develop into a good and safe shot, although it is impossible to shoot behind.

With the emphasis on outdoor sport, together with taking every opportunity to walk, my general health was excellent, but I still had to keep on my toes to guard against problems peculiar to paraplegics. The first of these was bed sores. Fortunately my skin tone was very good, and apart from one scare when I was in bed at Pinderfields I had no great trouble. The bladder was a more serious problem for me. Paraplegics are unable to empty the bladder because the brain's instructions to the relevant muscle cannot get through. I did my best to keep my urine retention as small as possible by utilising John Cook's patent trick of pressing on the prostate as frequently as possible, but even so I would get occasional infections in the bladder. For a few years after leaving Pinderfields I would return for check ups and also receive from the hospital my stores of gear which I needed to maintain discipline over my unruly bladder. This consisted primarily of a sheath or condom with a hole in it, a leg bag and a connecting spigot. Accidents were quite frequent in the early years, with consequent embarrassment, but I gradually became more skilled in its management and more diligent in the operation. My doctor sent me to a consultant urologist, Keith Yeates, who introduced me to a recent advance in technique. This consisted of an adhesive strip placed between the flesh of the penis and the sheath. Once I started using this device, it reduced the number of accidents enormously and gave me much more confidence when appearing in public. The bowel was also a problem, but by giving it particular attention and due respect, I managed to avoid anything other than a very rare accident.

I left Pinderfields wearing calipers which had been fitted on to my strongest shoes. These were held in the heel of the shoe and secured by velcro straps under the knee. They were extremely heavy and clumsy. If the velcro fastening should slip under my trousers where it could not be seen, there were disastrous consequences. This happened one day when I was fishing in Ireland in the rain, and was not discovered until I undressed in the bathroom. A huge wound had been opened up on my leg with the sandpaper-like velcro tearing my skin to ribbons. It took three months to heal. I was greatly relieved when I was eventually pointed in the direction of Lobbs of St James', the bootmakers, who proved quite equal to the task of stabilising my heels without a steel caliper. They developed a hidden strap, placed underneath the top of the boot and connecting the top of the toe cap to a strap around the top of the heel of the boot. This clever device kept the toe cap up and prevented the "brewers droop" which otherwise would have meant my loosely dangling toes hitting any pavement, kerb or step in my way. They made me boots, rather than shoes, in order to stabilise my ankles. Although they were very expensive I have never begrudged what I spent at Lobbs. It gave me immense pleasure to throw away those clumsy calipers.

As my strength returned so did my ability to walk longer distances and even to stand for periods of up to ten minutes or so. This enabled me to go to Northern Rugby Club and watch rugger matches, where I would deliberately take exercise by walking round from the clubhouse to the other side of the 1st XV pitch, sometimes even walking right round, stopping to stand and then walking on again for the length of a whole game, though more often I would seek sustenance in the clubhouse at half time! Most days I would have lunch at the Northern Counties Club which was about eight minutes' walk from my office and I relished this fresh air and exercise after a long morning at my desk in my wheelchair. Once I was driving myself into work, I would park the car in Dex Garage, situated next door to the office, from where the walk into the office only took me about five minutes. As I steadily grew in confidence as well as strength I used my car more to visit clients, friends and attend social functions.

To move further afield, particularly London, I had the choice of train or aeroplane. In the early 1970s the plane was much more user-friendly for disabled people, because wheelchairs were available easily at any airport, and staff at airports were also well-accustomed to handling disabled people. The London office car would meet me at London airport and I got to know successive chauffeurs quite well as they transported me to and from the City. The train was more difficult, although King's Cross terminal was much more convenient for the City than Heathrow. There were few wheelchairs in the stations and even fewer ramps. Baroness Masham used to travel regularly at that time from York to London and the station master at York knew full well he would get into trouble if he didn't have a set of ramps to get her on board. Since there was only one set for the North East line between York and Newcastle the chances for Peter Jowett (a disabled Price Waterhouse partner) or myself were pretty slim. Sometimes I had to travel in the guard's van in my wheelchair because it could not fit into the passenger compartments on the adjacent carriages. On one occasion a friendly steward brought me a gin and tonic from the bar to the guard's van! In the next decade, thanks partly to our lobbying, there was to be a change in attitude. Today I would think that disabled people are treated equally well at both stations and airports. Wheelchairs are now provided as a matter of course at railway stations and there is, in fact, far less hassle getting on to a train than there is when boarding a plane. In recent years I have noticed a large increase in the number of air travellers needing wheelchair assistance and this is adding to the hassle and creating inefficiency. Last year Sue and I were left behind in Capetown although I was in a wheelchair in the Club Class lounge.

In the summer of 1971 we all went to Majorca for a holiday, together with Sue's mother, who loved a hot climate. This was the first experience of flying abroad after my accident and it went well. We bumped into John and Christine Peart with their children on the plane and Derek and Pam Collings with their children (also called Nicola and Mark) were already on the island, so we had some very merry parties, particularly at the Mola Club which had a very steep funicular down to the level of the pool. I remember Tony and Derek having to manhandle me on their shoulders in and out of the funicular. Swimming was very good for me and it was generally easy to get into pools when the sun had dried the water splashes on the poolside, which otherwise would have caused my feet or sticks to slip. Indoor swimming pools can be a nightmare for disabled people on crutches for this very reason.

The following Easter we took the children to Paris by car and ferry and stayed in an amusing bed and breakfast place that advertised the fact that Casanova had slept there. One day I opted to spend the entire time in the Louvre, which not only had innumerable wheelchairs but also boasted a decent restaurant, while Sue took the children up the Eiffel Tower. Nicola, in particular, has never forgotten how she spurned this chance of seeing the art treasures of the Louvre – much to her regret in later years since she was to become a very talented and successful artist. In those days it was possible to drive reasonably safely around Paris, and park too, although I do recall that on one occasion we parked in Montmartre, returning a few hours later to discover that our car had been lifted bodily about ten yards. Fortunately it was quite unharmed. We bought a painting in Montmartre which has hung in my office ever since – a memento of a thoroughly enjoyable family holiday.

Whilst my car wheels might have been an extension of my legs, and gave me great independent mobility, I still needed my legs and crutches to get into many of the places which I had to visit, where it would have been impossible to use a wheelchair. Little thought was given, in those days, to access for the disabled. One instance I recall in particular was at the Accountants' Dinner at the Mayfair. I was dropped somewhat ignominiously at the back door of the hotel in my wheelchair, and taken via a labyrinth of kitchens and an exceptionally malodorous service lift to the banqueting hall. It was an unpleasant experience and one that I did not repeat, preferring in future to walk down innumerable staircases that seemed to last forever! As I was now quite strong and I was also fairly nimble on my crutches I was easily able to manage the occasional step or small staircase that many houses and offices seem to have specifically placed as obstacles for disabled people. Nevertheless, it was extremely heartening to know that when substantial improvements were made to the Theatre Royal in Newcastle the provision for disabled people was greatly improved. For my part I can now use a lift to ascend to the Grand Circle and higher floors which were previously barred to me.

Attitudes to disabled people, however, are more problematical, as the following little tale illustrates. I had parked my car in Hood Street near my Club, where there are several disabled spaces. On this occasion, all these spaces were full, although not all with cars carrying the "orange badge". I parked in a bay set aside for motor bikes, which was unoccupied – not surprising as it was mid-winter. There was another motor bike bay immediately opposite, also empty. On my return to my car – which was, of course, properly equipped with its orange badge – I was surprised to find a parking ticket. In vain did I search for the warden in order to remonstrate, so on my return home I wrote to the Chief Constable explaining the circumstances. I received no reply. In due course a summons arrived and I decided to fight the case. I rang the Chairman of Magistrates, whom I knew, and asked him how accessible the court was for a wheelchair.

"No trouble," he assured me. "There's a lift."

There was, indeed, a lift, as I discovered upon my arrival at court. I also discovered that the entrance to this lift was at the top of a flight of steps. Completely stuck, I had to prevail upon four burly policemen to hoist me and my wheelchair up the steps!

The tale ends happily. Apparently they had had great trouble trying to find a magistrate able to take the case as all available magistrates seemed to know me personally. When at last I arrived in court it was to discover that the official attitude had changed at the eleventh hour and the police case had been withdrawn. I was presented with a walkover!

It is important to take extra precautions with health when you are disabled and hygiene in relation to the bladder is particularly important. It is also helpful to try and avoid wounds in the area of the body that is paralysed because they take so long to heal. This was brought home to me forcibly once when at a party I sat on a radiator which I thought was turned off. However it must have been merely on a time switch and I did not feel the heat on my backside. The resulting burn took a year to heal and I still bear the scar twenty five years later.

Our social life returned fairly quickly to normal, my wheelchair being useful at home in enabling me to assist with preparations for dinner and supper parties, and clearing up afterwards. I soon worked out the best way to get in to my small wine cellar and I could command at least half of it from a sitting position on the staircase inside. I rarely took my wheelchair out with me if we were attending a function or going out to dinner because I could manage quite adroitly on my crutches and did not need to pour drinks. Someone else would do that. However it was very useful to have a high stool, perhaps a bar stool, made available to me if most of the guests at a function were standing. Nothing is more infuriating if you are disabled than everyone standing three feet higher than you are. Not only is it impossible too hear any conversation, but you also end up with a cricked neck straining to look up all the time. Eventually I bought my own cocktail stool – several, in fact – and I have had one placed in the Northern Counties Club for many years.

On my return home we placed an advertisement in the local paper, as follows:

FOR SALE: ONE SET OF GOLF CLUBS
WANTED: A GARDENER

Strangely, we got no purchasers for the golf clubs, which I gave away in the end, but we had sixteen prospective gardeners, one of whom helped Sue for some time. The garden is Sue's pride and joy, and she spends a lot of time planning and working in it. I was, at best, an assistant and after my accident was not much help. However, I did embark on a major construction exercise with the help of the children. There was a rockery outside the drawing room window with a reasonably flat level, gradually falling away down to the lawn. I decided to create two ponds, one on the upper and one on the lower level. which were fitted with liners and a water pump to provide a fountain and a waterfall and a return flow to the upper pond. Most of the work was executed by me sitting on my backside issuing instructions to Nicola and Mark. My engineering skills were clearly lacking because the system kept losing water. However, the effect was suitably decorative and we all felt triumphant. We planted lilies and other plants and after a successful expedition to the "hoppings" on the Town Moor three goldfish made their home in the bottom pond. Despite the attention of various predators, particularly the cat next door, they survived for several years, including being iced over every winter, until two of them disappeared one spring and the third mysteriously tripled in size.

I had learned how to paint in watercolours at school and with some time on my hands it seemed a fairly obvious pursuit to resurrect. It was moreover something that could be done from the boot of a car, so my disability was not much of a bar. My hesitant enthusiasm was given a very positive push forward by Irene Taylor who lived down the road. She was an expert artist, and determined to teach me the technique of oil painting so that I would have both of these traditional methods at my fingertips. She devoted a great deal of time to this task, for which I will be eternally grateful, for although I only kept up painting in oils for about three years it taught me a great deal, not only about that medium but about the respective merits of watercolours, gouache and acrylic, all of which I experimented with as a result of Irene's enthusiasm.

One thing that I had to come to terms with on my return from Pinderfields was my relationship with the different members of the family. Sue had been a rock from the moment that news of my accident had reached her and I had unhesitatingly leaned on her strength. When I came home for good we had to do a bit of getting to know each other again and she had to come to terms with the large variety of medical props that were now part of my life. Fortunately Jack Foster's worst forebodings about our sexual relationship did not come to pass and we have had a lot of satisfaction out of that side of our lives – as we have in so many other respects of our shared life together. It was wonderful for me to return to our house with its lovely garden and a wife who was so tremendously supportive in every aspect of my attempts to pick up the threads of my life. I am sure that the children were both affected by my accident but they did not talk about it much. I had always been very fond of my daughter Nicola and it was a bit of wrench when she went away to boarding school in 1971. I enjoyed immensely our visits to York to see her and take her out for trips into the lovely surrounding countryside. Mark seemed to have inherited my tendency to idleness and it was, therefore, something of a pleasant surprise when he passed his Common Entrance to Sedbergh in the summer of 1973. He had, however, already became a great companion to me in many ways, particularly enjoying coming with me on shooting and fishing trips.

I was able to enjoy the company of our dogs, Whisky the noisy border terrier, and Punch the large and unruly springer spaniel and they both made it clear, without any doubt, that they were glad to see me home again.

8

In Practice Again

My business is to create.
William Blake

 Y AMBITION IN THE SHORT TERM was to be able to pull my weight in the office and to take an active role once again in helping to push the firm forward. During the six months that I had been away various partners had covered for me but John Cooper had borne the brunt of the work. Most of my former clients were loyal and professed themselves happy with the service that they had received while I was away. What seemed extraordinary to me was the fact that they also appeared to be glad that I was back. John had got rid of one or two undesirable clients, and some he retained himself as he was building up his own portfolio at the time, but most of my original clients came back to me.

Malcolm drove me to the office every day, until such time as my car had been adapted and I had passed my driving test, and I was able to drive myself. I would clank into the office on my beastly calipers, which were concealed beneath my trousers – it would not have been quite so easy for a lady in a skirt! Peacocks produced a wheelchair so that I was reasonably mobile and able to carry my own files and other essential paraphernalia around with me. At first I did not keep regular office hours and I would still visit the University gym on a daily basis. Gradually, however, I increased my work rate and got back to my old habits, including the 7.00 am start. Fairly soon after my return, we acquired more space, because the office was expanding. John Cooper masterminded major alterations to the fourth floor which provided me with a new room near the lift, and us all with a new board room. I had hoped that a second lift would be installed to make life easier, since the sole lift the office boasted was grossly over-used and broke down frequently, leaving me either stranded on the ground floor or facing a climb of four flights. No such luck, however. Many a time I made the effort to climb the stairs, arriving exhausted at the top and venting my frustration on anyone who was unfortunate enough to get in my way.

In those days we had partners' meetings each month in the London office and I started travelling south on a regular basis, generally choosing to fly and being met at Heathrow by the London office chauffeur. This worked reasonably well but I had to do a lot of walking on my crutches which meant that by the end of the day I would be extremely weary. The Army and Navy Club was easily accessible; there was even a lift from the garage floor to the bedrooms and if necessary I would stay there overnight. However, staying on my own away from home was (and still is) a major exercise. If I was staying only one night I would try and get my overnight things into a small shoulder bag that I could carry (not without difficulty) if it proved necessary – which it often did. I had to have room for essential medical supplies and it was always a tight fit. In later years I was to travel abroad quite frequently as well as within the UK, so I became well-accustomed to the frustrations of air travel as a disabled person.

In November 1971 my father retired from the office. Although 68 years of age he was in good health and was to enjoy twelve years of very satisfying retirement, particularly as a much respected elder statesman of the Northumberland Golf Club, which was situated close to my parents' home. I took over, from him, the Secretaryship of the Northern Counties branch of the Institute of Directors and had seven very interesting years at the job before handing it on, in turn, to my partner Ken Patterson. I remember working closely with Gordon Carr, running the Institute's Forum at Newcastle University. By this time I was fully rehabilitated as a mainstream partner and my portfolio of clients was once again increasing.

The following year we started planning for the retirement of two more partners, Percy Cooper and John Pashley, and I can remember producing a strategic plan for Newcastle office, outlining specific roles for the partners and looking to materially increase the manager complement. It was generally felt that the partners were under too much pressure and needed to delegate more work to managers. In fact, it was not long before there were even more changes. In 1975 John Cooper went to Bristol to take charge of that office and David Smith came north from London to fill his shoes, but also with a national training role. Shortly after, we were joined by Peter Smith, our first full-time tax partner.

In 1972 Sue and I went to an Institute Conference in Majorca. Together with Joe and Rosemary Hurst from Liverpool we were representing Arthur Young McClelland Moores & Co at this prestigious meeting. Our luggage was lost at Majorca Airport. It contained most of my medical gear and life would have been extremely difficult had it not turned up after dinner!

The partners of Arthur Young, Torquay, 1973.

I also recall that it seemed impossible for the hotel to serve lunch in under three hours and the attendance at early afternoon meetings was understandably thin! At this conference we met David Lowry of Harmood Banner from Liverpool, who was there with his wife Rosemary and they both became firm friends. Denis Healey was one of the speakers. We had taken him out to supper the night before and he had talked very openly to us about a whole range of issues but I have to confess I did not recognise any of these views expressed when he spoke the next morning. A typical politician!

Each year in October we would have the Partners Annual Meeting. Most years these would take place at Turnberry or Gleneagles, although I can recollect one at Aviemore, to which Malcolm and I travelled by train across the Scottish Highlands, and one in 1973 at Torquay. This was a year prior to Percy's retirement. He was the Chairman of the Annual Meeting that year, and I travelled down with him in his car. It was the one occasion in the year when virtually all the partners (under 100 in the 1970s) were together, and we made much more of it than just an AGM. It was an exercise in what is now called "bonding" as well as an opportunity to scrutinise the inner workings and the strategy of the firm. We would also invite several of our American and other overseas colleagues to join us. We would work hard but also play hard, and not only at golf, although this was the sport favoured by the majority in the partnership. At Aviemore Lyndsay Gordon and I went fishing and I caught a nice fat trout which Judy Marchant, who was organising the meeting, had for breakfast. Michael Campbell Penny would traditionally lead the more energetically inclined on a long ramble over the Scottish fells. In the evening, after dinner, those who might have been dissatisfied with the decisions of the Partners Remuneration Committee would set about altering its composition at the card tables. I can remember on one occasion winning the last pot of the night at three card brag, which was worth £1000.

In the early seventies one or two of us (I can remember Gordon Howe joining me) sought to persuade our colleagues that we should be more ardent in our endeavours to build an Insolvency practice. This followed the national stature achieved by Robert Smith with his highly professional liquidation of Upper Clyde Shipbuilders. Having advocated this course of action, I felt that I had to put into practice what I was preaching. Thus in 1974 I took on my first substantial receivership, closely followed by two more. With an existing busy portfolio of audit and accountancy work, I was in a position to appreciate fully what hard work and tight deadlines meant. To help, I head-hunted a specialist insolvency manager, David Pallen, from London, and we worked very well together. When David moved back to London to join our insolvency department having failed to acclimatise to the frozen north, I acquired Alan Marlar from Peats in Manchester. Alan eventually became the insolvency partner in Newcastle, and David one of the partners in London.

Although in no sense could I be called a tax expert, for most of my time in practice I retained a working knowledge of tax as an enthusiastic amateur. On one occasion my prowess in tax affairs was put through a stern test. An old client of mine died. He had been a well-known Northumbrian bookmaker with a chain of shops throughout Northumberland, and a tin trunk containing about £10,000 in old white fivers was found in his house. The Revenue naturally sought to tax this "hoard" and refused to listen to my explanation that my client had won this money on a treble bet at Ayr while on a busman's holiday – which was his wont. He had no license to practise as a bookmaker in Scotland therefore I argued that his winnings were not part of his trade. Perhaps the Inspector did not believe this story at all. Anyway he made an assessment against which I appealed and requested that it be heard by the Special Commissioners. Peter Smith, who was by then our tax partner, tried to persuade me to use tax counsel, in accordance with the rules of our firm, but I wanted to take the case myself, partly because I knew the story to be true, partly because the dead client's son, who was now running the business, was my former articled clerk and I knew him to be as straight as a die, but mainly because I was curious to see just how I would perform. Peter helped me a great deal and in the event I dealt with the first four aspects of the appeal (which was where the money counted!) and Peter did the last, which was pure tax law. At the hearing we had to mount a very difficult staircase which caused some embarrassment to the Revenue. The Inspector put me in the dock and cross-questioned me about the business and its accounts. I suspect he was trying to trip me up, but his action was counter-productive. At the end of the day I won all my four appeals ... but Peter lost his.

As you grow older in the profession it is natural that more people will come across you in a professional capacity. Word of mouth is by far the best advertisement, and if you have done a good job for someone they will inevitably talk about you to their friends and colleagues. In this way you will not only increase your number of clients but also establish a good reputation throughout your region or your speciality. Our aim was to grow our practice by these means and it is interesting to reflect upon the origins of some of our work. An accidental meeting in a train, a friendly bank director making an introduction, or a chance remark at a dinner party have all been responsible for some our new clients. Later we were to get into the business of proposing for work in a beauty parade against other accountants, which meant that we would all have to sharpen up on our presentation skills. Although I didn't mind that, I always preferred a one to one situation with a potential client, where I could explain fully my point of view and use my powers of persuasion.

Developing the practice called for dexterity in maximising contacts and situations. One particularly interesting and enjoyable one was when I advised a small group who were putting together a bid for the North East Television franchise. Ken Lister, from our Bradford office, introduced me to some TV professionals who had bright ideas for a North East franchise and I in turn introduced them to Paul Nicholson, (now Sir Paul) chairman of Vaux Breweries who put together a group including, *inter alia*, Tom Cowie and Diana Eccles. I helped when we made our presentation to the IBA and happened to meet George Russell (later Sir George) on the London train a few days later who told me that our presentation had been outstanding. We did not win the franchise but Paul joined the Tyne Tees Television board as vice chairman.

In 1975 I was elected to the Executive Committee of Arthur Young and

In the USA, *circa* 1975.

was to serve for the next nine years. The Executive Committee consisted, at that time, of a Chairman, John Darby, and five elected members – Gordon Howe, Gordon Anderson, Joe Hurst, Dick Anderson and myself, with an Administrative Partner, Ian Ogle, and it ran the firm, appointing managing partners to each office and region, deciding on priorities for growth and expenditure and creating the strategy for the future. The meetings were regular and quite intensive – certainly one and a half days was normal. And we moved all over the country. It was hard work, but exhilarating in many ways and I established a great rapport with my fellow members. I also met partners from other offices on a more regular basis than I would have done had I been confined to my office in Newcastle all this time. I realised the responsibility that I assumed but it did not depress me. In fact I think I rather revelled in it. At the same time I had to keep on top of my professional work, my busy and expanding insolvency practice, my audit and general accountancy practice and also play my part in the development of the Newcastle office.

In the time I was on the Executive Committee we made a number of minor mergers. I was particularly involved in the acquisition of the Bradford-based firm of R S Dawson, which was to form the basis of our Yorkshire office. We were one of the last of the big eight accountancy firms to have a base in Yorkshire. The big merger, however, was with

Joselyn Leighton Bennett in 1981, a move which brought in over fifty partners and materially increased the size of the firm. I travelled abroad on Executive Committee business on various occasions, particularly to the United States to meet with our colleagues on the Arthur Young US Management Committee. On those occasions Sue would accompany me. Another time I went to California with Ian Ogle, the Administrative Partner of the firm, to attend a world wide conference. After this meeting we had planned to drive from San Francisco to Los Angeles where we each had a client to visit. However, our sojourn happened to coincide with a time of considerable unrest in the western half of the United States. When people began shooting one another in petrol queues we were advised to get out of San Francisco quickly. We finished up in Las Vegas where we dined with Raquel Welch and saw the Grand Canyon, and I taught my Scots Presbyterian friend Ian Ogle to play roulette. It was a memorable visit!

What was my role as a partner in Arthur Young? First and foremost a partner is an ambassador for the firm. It is primarily by his or her actions and behaviour that the firm will be judged. I always felt this most keenly. Secondly, I was a mainstream partner serving on the Executive Committee, therefore involved in the firm's strategic planning and development. Thirdly, I was a partner in Newcastle office, with a minor involvement in the administration of the office but a wider involvement in the development of the firm in the North East business community. Finally, but most importantly, I was involved as a General Practitioner in insolvency, audit, accountancy and giving general business advice to my clients, large and small.

9

Disability North

Tell them, that, to ease them of their griefs ...
... in life's uncertain voyage I will some kindness do them
William Shakespeare

 HORTLY AFTER MY RETURN from Pinderfields in 1971 I was
asked to join a discussion about setting up a coordinating,
service-providing body for disabled people. This was one of
several meetings which took place only two doors away from
my home, where Graham Grant lived. He was the University doctor and
had been asked to chair a steering committee by the Northumberland
Tyneside Council for Social Service. Graham's wife Jo was part of the
group, as was Mari Lynn, who also lived in Graham Park Road.

We were joined by Peter Jowett, a partner in Price Waterhouse, who
had had polio shortly after qualifying as a chartered accountant. The idea
was to build an organisation of excellence that would provide help and
advice for disabled people, their families and carers. At the time there
was nothing like this in the North East, although London already boasted
RADAR and the Disablement Income Group, with which Mari was heavily
involved. With the support of Newcastle upon Tyne City Social Services
Committee we set up the Newcastle Council for the Disabled in September
1972, with twenty seven members. Our income in the first year totalled
a mere £4,300: a grant of £4,000 from the Social Services Committee and
three individual donations of £100.

The Newcastle upon Tyne Council for the Disabled was originally set
up under deed and later formed into a company limited by guarantee
with rather wider objectives in order to make it easier for us to build and
own property, and I recollect a long and rather acrimonious correspondence with the Charity Commissioners in connection with the change in
status. Graham Grant was our first chairman, I was elected vice-chairman
and Peter was the honorary treasurer. In 1973 we held our first exhibition
and established a swimming club, and the following year we moved in
to Mea House in Ellison Place, where Alfred Morris MP, Minister for the

Disabled, opened our first professional service: an Aids Centre. This was not only a permanent exhibition of aids to daily living, but also a centre offering practical advice and assistance through the professional skills of our staff, who were mainly occupational therapists. We owed much to the help and influence of Brian Roycroft, Newcastle's Director of Social Services, in developing the concept and getting Alf Morris to open it. The staff of the Aids Centre were led by Olive Jeff and it rapidly assumed an important teaching role, which it still fulfils today, although its title has now changed to The Disabled Living Centre. By 1979 the Centre was handling over 4000 visitors per year. Today it has many more.

In 1975, the Information and Advisory Service was started under Angela Blenkinsop, with the objective of handling any enquiry from, or on behalf of, disabled people. This would include information on mobility benefits, DHSS grants and allowances, services provided by voluntary and statutory agencies, housing problems, recreational facilities, employment, education, access holidays and myriad other questions. By 1979 the service was handling over 1500 enquiries a year and now the figure is well over 5000. Many were by telephone but a good proportion (about a quarter) were personal callers, sometimes without appointment. We launched an appeal to raise funds from the voluntary sector to help to pay for the running of our services since, even at this stage, it was becoming clear that government and local authority funding would not cover our costs. The services were used by many voluntary and statutory organisations which existed to help disabled people, as well as disabled individuals themselves, their carers and their families. Our reputation was spreading rapidly, creating an increasing demand for the services we were providing. A spiral was developing which made cost containment ever more difficult.

We embarked on a Speech After Stroke project, as a result of which a number of Speech After Stroke Clubs were successfully established, and became an integral part of the rehabilitation scene in the North East. In 1976 we started the Volunteer Drivers Group to help those who were unable to use public transport and who would otherwise be completely housebound. Many lasting friendships were formed between drivers and passengers and this valuable service was to last over ten years, by which time the general mobility of disabled people had improved to such an extent that demand was greatly reduced. In 1978 we mounted a major "access" initiative and published *The Ins and Outs of Newcastle*, which filled a heartfelt need. Sadly we could not afford to update and reprint this publication regularly, despite the demand. We received a DHSS grant which enabled us to establish the Continence Advisory Service, which broke completely new ground in an area where there was an enormous amount of ignorance. Much of the time of Helen White, who became our principal advisor, was spent training health professionals, specifically continence nurse advisors, and over the next fifteen years a network of trained advisors was built up throughout the region. Around this time, Christine Tarling took over as our principal OT. A little later Angela Blenkinsop retired and was succeeded as Senior Information Officer by Mary Kelly. Both were admirably supported by Jean Nicklin. In 1980 Peter Jowett took over the chairmanship of the Council from Graham Grant, although I remained as vice chairman.

Nineteen eighty one was the International Year of Disabled People and I was asked to chair the North East committee, with a brief to maximise its impact. In launching the Year, I described it as "... a unique opportunity for organisations and the general public to improve the lives of disabled people. The success of the year will depend on the willingness of everyone to take initiatives, both locally and nationally, to increase awareness of the needs and the abilities and aspirations of disabled people ...". The response from sports clubs, schools, churches, organisations, individuals and the media led to the initial fulfilment of the objectives I had outlined and there is no doubt that public awareness of disability was dramatically raised. I was determined that it should not be allowed to drop back and since 1981 we have worked hard to maintain a high profile.

The high point of the year was the visit of HRH The Prince of Wales to open our "Learning for Living" Exhibition. As Patron of the International Year he showed a tremendous interest in, and knowledge of, the problems of disability. The exhibition was visited by 2500 people and was the largest event in terms of organisation that we had attempted thus far. Its theme drew together the two strands of education and rehabilitation and for the first time an effort was made to bring the advantages of employing disabled people to the attention of potential employers.

By 1983, we were running out of space in Mea House and we were determined to try to build our own premises. At the end of that year we purchased about two acres of land near the Freeman Hospital but we needed to raise some £900,000 to fund the new, special-purpose building. We were extremely fortunate to receive £600,000 from the Regional Health Authority and Joint Local Authority funding. This was made possible largely because of the involvement of Graham and Jo Grant with Joint Planning, bringing our work to the notice of senior health service administrators, together with the continuing interest of Brian Roycroft who chaired the Joint Planning team. Peter Jowett and I led the appeal which raised the rest, largely from trusts and companies. On a cold, blustery day in January 1984 Peter and I joined Arthur Taylor, chairman of Newcastle Health Authority to dig the first sod of earth. In fact, we were able to keep £150,000 in reserve after we moved in to the new building, which we called the Dene Centre and which was superbly designed by Mari Lynn's husband Jack. The building gave us all the room we wanted and was opened by HRH Duchess of Gloucester on 17 October 1985. When we moved in to our new home we were able to make room for the Communication Aid Centre, which was run by Newcastle Health Authority. It was one of six such centres in the country, designed to help people who had problems with communication, for example severely impaired speech, and the inability to communicate feelings or ideas. There were many areas of overlap with other centres, so the Dene Centre became a natural home for the CAC.

For some years we had been concerned that our name, The Newcastle upon Tyne Council For The Disabled, was too much of a mouthful and was also too parochial. In later years we adopted Disability North as our trading name, but at the time of moving into our new building we decided that in order to raise awareness we would emphasise the name of the building in all our literature. As a result The Dene Centre is well known today throughout the region as the centre of excellence for all matters concerned with disability.

In 1986 Peter Jowett sadly died. I took over the chairmanship of the Council with Mari Lynn as my vice chairman. The Dene Centre was busier than ever but a lack of money was starting to loom large as one of our major problems. I invited our founder, Graham Grant, to undertake a review of our task load: not only to ascertain exactly what we *were* doing, but also what we *should* be doing. We had set up a Policy and Planning Committee which was to recommend where our resources should be concentrated. At the time, all decisions were taken by an Executive Committee which met quarterly. This was a slow and cumbersome process and, in order to increase efficiency, I established a small management group which met regularly with the Director and other key employees, thus enabling decisions to be taken more quickly. My general aim was somehow to improve and also steady our rather rocky funding base which was constantly at the mercy of government cut backs. Unfortunately I was not wholly successful in achieving this aim. Simon Hogg had been appointed our first fund-raiser in 1983/4 and I worked closely with him to try and increase funding from the private sector. We did meet with some success in this sphere. When I was appointed a non-executive member of the Northern Regional Health Authority I was in a better position to see that our health related grants bore some comparison to our costs. Although this was a small success we were unable to achieve anything other than maintained support from Local Authorities which was way below the cost of the services we were providing. In the four years leading up to 1992 our reserves dropped from £250,000 to £150,000 and they were destined to fall still further, to around £100,000. Those years were a very difficult period indeed in terms of financial management for the Dene Centre. I am very much relieved to know that today the reserves are rising once again.

Meanwhile, changes were taking place. Professor Mike Barnes, our first Professor of Rehabilitation in the North East, joined the Dene Centre in 1988 and became vice chairman, and Kevin Durkin joined us as Director of Education and Client Services. Our Director Donald Dempsey had been with us for most of our brief history but when, in 1990, he left us, Kevin took over as Chief Executive. We were extremely lucky at that time to have Lynne Sandals, Mary Kelly and Helen White as our Principal OT, Senior Information Officer and Continence Advisor respectively. Our services remained – and still remain – in demand as much as ever and one of the reasons that we are a centre of excellence is because of the quality of our people.

In August 1992 I resigned as chairman, and Bill Midgley took over the post. However, that was not the end of the story. Some time after handing over the the chair, I was invited to become a vice president of the Newcastle Council for the Disabled. I was greatly honoured to join Lord Walton, Graham Grant and Mari Lynn, and later to be joined by Maureen Taylor. In this capacity I still support Disability North in whatever way I can, attending as many executive meetings as possible. Specifically, I assist Richard Walton who is now in charge of fundraising, and offer advice and practical help in topping and tailing appeal letters if I happen to be well known to the intended recipient. Appeals have become much more sophisticated of late, mainly because a lot of the financing of the Dene Centre is now project based. Lynne Sandals and Mary Kelly have done a fine job and there is a great spirit amongst all those who work for Disability North. I take every opportunity I can to promote the organisation, which is the centre of excellence for disability in the North East in the private sector. The success of its Disabled Living Exhibition at Gateshead in recent years is a good example of its fine current achievements.

I am aware that I have not mentioned more than a fraction of the members of staff, volunteers or committee members with whom I worked, but I have many happy memories of being part of a dedicated and enthusiastic team and of helping to build a great success story.

10

The Calvert Trust

The name of Calvert, it shall live
If words of mine can give it life
William Wordsworth

N 1974 JOHN FRYER-SPEDDING asked me to help him with an enterprise he wanted to start in the Lake District. His plan was to build an outdoor activity centre for disabled people, providing them with the opportunity to enjoy and appreciate that wonderful countryside. I agreed readily and went over to Keswick to meet John and hear more about his plans. He and his family were proposing to give to a newly formed Trust two farmhouses – Little Crosthwaite, adjacent to Bassenthwaite Lake, and Old Windybrowe, near Keswick. With some fund raising, and particularly with the help of the government's Job Creation Scheme to provide employment, the farmhouses could be adapted for disabled people and we could employ instructors to teach them to sail and ride and partake in all manner of outdoor pursuits which they would otherwise be unable to enjoy. It was a brilliant concept and I wholeheartedly entered into the planning. I asked John what he proposed to call this new Trust, and he told me the following story:

Some two hundred years previously, that same stretch of land between Keswick and Bassenthwaite which John now owned had been owned by John's forbear, Raisley Calvert, who had grown up with William Wordsworth. Wordsworth and his sister Dorothy had struggled to make ends meet. While they were at school together and afterwards, Calvert let Wordsworth live rent free in Old Windebrowe and when, in his early twenties, Calvert lay dying, Wordsworth nursed him devotedly. In his will, Calvert left £900 to Wordsworth, who was to immortalise his friend's name in *The Prelude*: "The name of Calvert, it shall live, if words of mine can give it life …". In order to fulfil Wordworth's prophecy, and also to reflect the spirit of mutual help portrayed in this remarkable slice of family history, John suggested that we call our new organisation The Calvert Trust. The name lives on today.

And so we began, slowly at first but with gathering momentum. The first guests arrived in 1977 and the following year the centre was officially opened by His Grace the Duke of Buccleuch, who had broken his back in a riding accident. On the day of the opening, His Grace, severely disabled as he was, drove alone all the way from London, proving just what disabled people can do. Elinor, Viscountess Rochdale was a key player from the start, not just as our first chairman of trustees and of the management committee, but also through her indomitable determination to make things happen. Norman Croucher, the double amputee climber, was one of the first trustees. He, too, provided great inspiration by virtue of his own exploits.

John Spedding made further gifts to the trust of a boathouse on the lakeside and an adjacent wood, which now houses a nature trail. More and more groups of disabled people were using the centre and returning each year. By 1979 it was all going so well that the trustees, together with the Newcastle Council for the Disabled, asked me to chair a working party to look at possible sites on the east of the Pennines for a second Calvert Trust centre. John joined the working party, together with Peter Jowett and, *inter alia*, Matthew Festing who was extremely active in the TA and who was most helpful in planning and accessing the forest trails. Dick Gaisford and John North-Lewis both gave us great help in their respective capacities as Land Agent and Lawyer, and we also had the services of Stan Calvert, Newcastle University's Head of Outdoor Recreation – no relation of Raisley but one whose surname provided a happy coincidence. We looked at various sites but the new man-made lake at Kielder, then under construction, seemed to have so many advantages and was clearly the favourite. It did, however, have one problem: midges. I held up our report for almost a year while we consulted extensively with the locals and the workmen who were building the dam, before concluding that on most days the midge was unlikely to prove a major problem other than at dawn and at dusk, at which times of day our guests would normally be safely inside. Furthermore, as our Centre was sited in a wind funnel, the midge was much less likely to be a nuisance. We were extremely fortunate to be able to enter into an alliance with Northumberland County Council, who operated their field study centre from a farmhouse called Low Cranecleugh, near the shore up the Whickhope Burn. It helped greatly that Peter and I knew Michael Trollope, the Director of Education of the County Council (who also lived in Graham Park Road!) and it was agreed that we could build a purpose-designed centre immediately adjacent to their farmhouse. We also consulted the locals before launching a new centre on their doorstep. John Charlton, of Hesleyside Hall, who had

H.M. The Queen visits the Calvert Trust at Kielder.

strongly opposed the concept of a reservoir at Kielder, only approved of the Calvert Trust concept once the lake was a *fait accompli*. He kindly hosted a reception in his home so that we could explain our ideas to the local community. It was now all coming together and our report was accepted both by the trustees and the Council. The way ahead was clear and we were all set to commence work on our second Calvert Trust centre in Northumberland.

I was asked to be the first chairman of the management committee of the new Trust, which was called The Northumbria Calvert Trust. I was immensely pleased when Sir Ralph Carr-Ellison, an influential figure in the North East, agreed to become chairman of trustees. Within a very short time we had a local hard core of trustees comprising Elizabeth, Duchess of Northumberland, John Charlton, Professor Sir John Walton,

Dean of Newcastle University Medical School, Eve Dudding, Michael
Pyman and Ted Wrangham, with Norman Croucher and Ken Roberts,
the national disabled sailing coach, as our outside professionals. Peter
Goodinson, who was seriously disabled with a back injury, became vice
chairman of the management committee – he and I had played rugger
twenty five years earlier and we worked well together. He lived near
Hesleyside and was therefore conveniently close at hand. Peter proved to
be a tower of strength throughout the ensuing years.

In November 1981 we launched our appeal, the target being to raise
£750,000. However, when construction work commenced it was discovered that we were building on boggy ground. A raft had to be created to
provide a stable base and the extra costs meant that we had to raise our
target to £1 million. Unlike Keswick, we had no Job Creation Scheme to
help, so we had to pay the going rate for a first-class building operation.
Jack Lynn was our architect and once again did a splendid job. We raised
the £1 million thanks to the generosity of many good friends. The Rank
Foundation, who had already supported Keswick, were magnificent and
loyally took us through that first hurdle of increasing the target. Their
support was matched by Billy Leech, to whom I had spoken about the
project sometime before Christmas. When I next met him, just before
Christmas Day, he told me that he would give us a very substantial
donation. I had formed a small appeal group which included David Ridley
of Park End, then High Sheriff of Northumberland, and David Wilson,
a partner in Peats. David (Wilson) had a good knowledge of the Welton
Trust, having worked on it in his London office, and he set up a meeting
in London so that we could talk to the trustees there. We worked up a
Box and Cox routine on the breakfast train and went in to bat in some
exclusive City office. We were certainly put through the mill and cross-
questioned in detail about the project, but emerged with a grant of £75,000
– well worth the trip south! I wrote a personal note to the Chairmen of
The Times top 1000 companies. To my surprise, most replied, more often
than not with a cheque. (I wonder whether the same action would bear
similar fruit today?) The Countryside Commission, Sports Council and
Tourist Board all produced reasonable grants. By the end of 1983 we had
raised our £1 million, and had paid for a most wonderful building.

The management committee now embarked on the task of running the
centre. We were lucky in finding Simon and Loveday Spencer, who had
some time on their hands. Simon was a great help on the hotel side of
things, and Loveday proved equally useful on the house. Christine Tarling
brought her expertise as an OT to the committee and Derek Craven
addressed the problems of management with his Durham University

background. Jim Wainwright had been the warden for the County Council's Field Study Centre, and we made him joint warden for the whole project, with a Calvert Trust Chief Instructor responsible to him for the Calvert Trust activities. Peter Goodinson was invaluable as my number two, because he lived much closer to the cntre than I did and was on hand to sort out the myriad details that had to be attended to throughout the building phase and in setting up the new operation. In the summer of 1984 Sue and I took a party of young people (including our son Mark) to stay for a long weekend in order to put the new facilities to the test. We had a wonderful time, but did encounter some practical problems: Sue, for example, was unable to climb into the upper bunk in our room because there was no handrail. However, all these minor details were seen to and shortly thereafter we were officially opened by HRH Princess Alexandra. The second Calvert Trust was in business.

In the ensuing years the number of disabled visitors to Kielder steadily increased and we slowly improved the facilities. There were additional appeals to raise money to build a new international size riding centre and, later, three chalets and instructors' accommodation. Michael Pyman undertook to raise funds for his family to purchase steel, which the apprentices of Swan Hunter yard at Hebburn turned into pieces of a climbing tower, which in turn was built by the TA Royal Engineers at the Centre. It was christened "Zonk's Mountain" in memory of Mike's brother who was killed on D Day, and it was officially opened in the presence of many of his ex-Para comrades by two of our trustees: Norman Croucher, our legless climber, and Sir Ranulph Fiennes, the explorer, who had a race up to the top of the tower. In 1986 Sir Ralph Carr-Ellison stood down as chairman of trustees and I was asked to assume the position, with Peter Goodinson becoming chairman of the management committee. Peter Lloyd and Simon Spencer became joint vice chairmen. It was necessary for Peter Goodinson and I to communicate quite frequently and one of our favourite ways of doing so was to fish together up at Kielder. I remember one day we thought we would exercise some new shortwave radios which had been given to the centre. We radioed for help from the middle of the lake and were most gratified when our request for additional supplies of liquid refreshment were brought out to us by the rescue boat! Balancing income and expenditure was a constant battle but gradually the advantage of our partnership with the County Council began to pay off and we started to inch within sight of a break even, which Keswick had been achieving for some time.

In 1988, Jim Wainwright's contract came to an end and it was decided that we needed to upgrade the position of director, because the Calvert

A fund-raising Evening of Music with Sir Ralph Carr-Ellison (Chairman of Trustees at Kielder) and Elizabeth, Duchess of Northumberland.

Trust was now becoming quite a complicated business. We advertised the post and, in spite of hitting the central postal strike, we had nearly one hundred applicants. The job specification for the post included the following criteria:

  i. The successful applicant should be used to working with disabled people

  ii. He or she should be a proven leader and capable of inspiring loyalty in the staff

  iii. He or she should have reached a high standard in at least one of our outdoor activities

  iv. He or she should have some business experience

  v. Some hotel experience would be desirable

Among the applicants was Peter Cockerill; a former monk, Peter had worked all his life with disabled people and had taken parties of disabled to Lourdes. At the age of 26 he had been made the youngest Housemaster at Worth Public School. He was an experienced mountaineer and had made a solo ascent of the Matterhorn. Two years before, he had been given leave to be seconded to the business world and was currently an under-manager at the Royal Scot Hotel. With such a close mirror-image of the job specification it was hardly surprising that Peter was appointed, even from a very strong field of candidates.

As we moved into the nineties the Calvert Trust, with its two operating centres, had gained the reputation of being a very dynamic organisation. Visitors came from all over the country and abroad although the majority at Kielder were from Scotland and the north of England. Already our thoughts were turning to the south.

In 1990, following several expeditions to Exmoor led by John Spedding, we were able to acquire the freehold of Wistlandpound Farm for £370,000. An anonymous donor had come up with £100,000 and we managed to raise the rest from some of the loyal grant making trusts who had supported us in the past. Wistlandpound was north east of Barnstaple on the edge of the National Park and came with forty acres of land. It was adjacent to a reservoir which belonged to South West Water. The first task was to put together a properly representative body of trustees and a local management group. Sir John Palmer, a former President of the Law Society who had retired to that part of the world, was the first chairman of the trustees, followed by Edwin Beckett, a retired General who was Director of Corporate Affairs for Grand Met. We were extremely lucky to have tremendous commitment from John Dornton, one of my partners in Arthur Young who had moved from London to the Bristol office. Although still quite a distance from Exmoor he gave a lot of time to the project and took a major responsibility for the first tranche of fundraising. This was £250,000 which we got with the help of personal and charitable trust donations, grants from the Rural Development Commission and the Foundation for Sport and the Arts. We converted the farmhouse adequately in order to take small numbers of disabled people on a self-catering basis. The children from West Buckland school nearby challenged Aneka Rice to provide us with a boathouse. The "Challenge Aneka" team went into action one wet weekend in 1993, converting a traditional stone building by the reservoir into a new boathouse, building the road, a floating jetty and a path for wheelchairs from the Centre down to the lake.

Nell, Countess of Arran was the vice chairman of trustees and a great strength, particularly taking the chair of the appeal committee when we had to launch the big appeal in order to convert the old farm buildings we had acquired into a fully equipped Calvert Trust centre, which we did in 1994. Peter Steel masterminded a most professional campaign which raised £3.9 million over the next two years. The quadrangle of Victorian farm buildings was converted to provide *en suite* accommodation for seventy people, including four self-contained family flats; a kitchen, dining room and conservatory were on the ground floor and were complemented by a large function room, bar and reception lounge above (where we used to hold extremely draughty trustees meetings before the conversion work had begun!). We built a substantial swimming/hydrotherapy pool and covered riding school, games hall and stables as well as an outdoor climbing wall. By th nd of 1996, the project was complete. The centre director, Mike Wagemakers, has worked hard getting his small staff up to scratch. Already the order book is growing and, with its naturally fine position on the edge of Exmoor, I have no doubt about the future success of our latest centre.

Although the Calvert Trust has now passed its twenty-first birthday and maintains three operating centres, it is only recently that these centres have been formally linked through a Council, of which I am the chairman, which provides a focal point for discussion and consultation and facilitates the sharing of ideas and experience, thus enabling the centres to fulfil their missions more effectively. We were all thrilled when we were awarded the Lord Hunt Award in 1995, "for outstanding acheivement and endeavour in increasing human well-being and goodwill through outdoor activities" and Lord Hunt told us that the Calvert Trust had given a sense of achievement and purpose which many people without disabilities take for granted. The Calvert Trust is all about enriching the lives of disabled people and over the last two decades we have helped many disabled people live a fuller life. The fundamental principle which guides the organisation is concentrating on what disabled people *can* do, not on what they cannot do, and I look to the future with confidence. Recently we visited Lourdes in the Pyrenees with a view to considering whether a fourth Calvert Trust might be situated in that part of France. Who knows what the future has in store for this exciting organisation?

11

All Work And No Play . . .

The Gods do not deduct from man's
allotted span the hours spent fishing.
Babylonian Proverb

F ALL INDEPENDENT SPORTS accessible to disabled people, fishing from a boat must be one of the best. It helps to have someone to assist when getting into the boat, if only to steady it when you sit on the gunnel and lean back to slide on to the thwart but, once all your gear is to hand and you are safely in position, you really do not need much help at all. Cushion, rod, spare rod, net, fishing bag, hat, picnic basket, spare waterproofs: all must be transported from car to boat, which can prove quite a complex manoeuvre when you need both hands on your crutches. I have developed a way of dealing with this problem which I use at Hallington Lakes, and which might be used anywhere you can get a Range Rover or similar vehicle down to the lakeside. First of all, I reverse the car to the water's edge. Then, unhooking the boat's securing rope if necessary, I sit on the tailgate and pull the boat from the mooring in to the side so that it is only a couple of feet or so away from the vehicle. I can then transfer all the gear directly from car to boat myself. Once in the boat your legs are not much use other than as a bit of ballast and as a means of balancing yourself on the thwart. If you have normal upper body strength as, luckily, I do, you can row as well as any able-bodied fisherman. Rowing is an excellent form of exercise although admittedly now that I am well into my sixties I do get tired on windy days. Many fishermen nowadays use electric outboards but I could not cope with the weight of the battery, let alone the motor. I do, however, benefit from a second position in the boat – I place a swivel seat on the adjacent thwart, and I can easily manoeuvre myself, with my arms on the gunnels, to that seat when I have finished rowing and the boat is on a drift.

I have fished with friends all my life but I can still enjoy fishing on my own. There is a peace and quiet to be found in such solitude, and time

Fishing at John Browne-Swinburne's trout lake at Capheaton with Peter Goodinson.

passes without notice as you pit your wits against the infuriating trout who never behave as expected, and *never* do the same thing twice. If the fishing is very quiet you have a unique opportunity to 'stand and stare', and just forget the cares of the world. However, it must be said that the best remembered days are those spent in the company of a friend or two. Tony Peart, Peter Goodinson, John Baxter and Maurice Lowther all fished with me over the years and the fishing tales I could tell would fill a book. Fishing with Peart at Crookfoot near Hartlepool was a particular joy, being ghillied by Mr Jewel and grossly overfed by his wife, with the best fishing normally reserved for the evening rise. Maurice, Tony and I had some memorable days at Colt Crag and Crag Lough in Northumberland. On one of the latter occasions Maurice fell in, and we had a terrible job getting him back on board. Tony and I once met for lunch at The George at Chollerford, on a gloriously sunny day in July. I recollect that we bumped into Jimmy Woodeson who was, at the time, entertaining some Chinese visitors who seemed to be enraptured by the gardens. After an excellent lunch Tony and I went to Crag Lough and dapped with live and artificial daddies. By the time Sue arrived with a picnic supper we had filled the boat with fish, with time enough for Sue to fish the evening rise herself. John Browne-Swinburne has often very kindly invited us to fish his lake at Capheaton, where we *had* to fish from a boat. I have a mounted

Catching a salmon on the Loch Choire Estate with Derek Knowles.

4lb trout dated 1977 to remind me permanently of the joys of fishing there. Mark caught his first big trout there at about that time. I also took him to Currerevagh in Ireland, one August when he was 18 and we dapped with grasshoppers which our ghyllie Parr Molloy bred in his garden.

The best fishing I can remember though, has been at Loch Choire in Sutherland where Derek Knowles has often invited Sue and me, and sometimes Mark, to fish, generally in June. The first time I fished for trout there on Loch Truderscraig in the mayfly season we hit gold – 114 trout between three of us. Since then Sue and I have got over one hundred more than once, and several times eighty or over. Yet it never seems that you are catching too many fish. There are long spells when the lake goes flat. I prefer to fish dry fly in those conditions, with an imitation mayfly, grey wulff or an invicta.

The Mallart flows for three or four miles through the estate from Loch Choire to the River Naver and, if in spate, Derek would take me down the river in an Argocat to one of the pools where there might be a salmon. It is necessary to stalk the salmon on a narrow spate river like the Mallart because there is very little cover. So it is no great hardship for me to don waterproof trousers and to crawl with my rod down the pool. I remember on another occasion taking my Range Rover to the Bridge pool where I expected to find a salmon. I was on my own and I had a walk of about fifty yards from the car to a high bank (fifteen feet) just below the bridge. I crawled the last few yards through heather so that I wouldn't be seen, and peered over the parapet. There was no sign of a fish. I prepared myself and cast into the waterfall just below the bridge. The fly went rushing downstream with the current but my line snagged on a rock and I gave a sharp tug to free it. A salmon rose at the bottom of the pool and cleared my line for me. He had taken the fly, and my tug had hooked him! Then began a great fight. I had a 4lb cast on my little trout rod and the salmon dashed all over the place. After about twenty minutes I had coaxed him up under my bank and, with a quick backward flick, he rushed onto a tiny bit of shingle immediately below me. The fly dropped out of his mouth and he started to wriggle back to the water. I threw myself over the bank and landed on top of him, grabbed a stone and finished him off – then pondered what to do next. I threw the salmon up the bank but it did not reach the lip and merely slithered all the way down again. Next time I threw it further, and it landed safely in the heather. Then I had to get myself up the slippery bank, with no crutches. On my hands and knees it took me a full ten minutes, and I arrived at the top triumphant but absolutely whacked. It would have made highly entertaining viewing for anyone watching with a cine camera! Later that week Sue caught a salmon herself, so we both had something to celebrate.

One of the most natural sports, apart from fishing, must be grouse shooting. Grouse, unlike pheasant, are a truly wild bird and have never been reared by man, although many have tried. Grouse shooting is rather challenging from a sitting position because they generally fly low and swinging is much easier on a high bird. But I relish the challenge of grouse, and love a day on the moor.

Elsewhere I have described how my shooting progressed, following the accident, using the Land Rover with a swivel seat mounted on the back. Over the years I have had a specially adapted Land Rover with a V8 engine (not very reliable) and several Range Rovers. The back seat folded down, and a large electric sun roof was fitted. I had to walk from the driving seat to the tailgate, manoeuvre myself into the back of the vehicle, open the roof and climb, not without some difficulty, on to the chair. Most of the upper part of my body was then outside. On occasion I would act as a walking gun, with somebody driving the vehicle. The disadvantages were extreme wear and tear on my shoulders from hauling myself on to the

Shooting at Wolsingham.

seat, the fact that the interior of the car got completely soaked in rainy weather, and that the sun roof was prone to rust after about three years. I have now progressed to a chair fitted with a spike which slots in to an adapted bull bar at the front of the car; the advantages being that once the chair has been put in place at the start of the shooting day, all I have is a short walk to the front of the car, and my feet remain on the ground. I can therefore drive to my stand and be reasonably independent. A recent innovation is an ATV – a four-wheeled motorbike with a disabled seat on the back, which is very well suited to the terrain on grouse moors and provides me with a great measure of mobility.

In the 1970s I was shooting rather badly, so I went to see Ron Sowerby, the famous shooting coach who lived near Harrogate. He pointed out that my left eye had taken over as the 'master eye' and since I shoot off my right shoulder this was bad news. He taught me to shut my left eye while shooting and he also fitted my guns for me – I had just bought a pair of beautiful Papes from Michael Pybus. After a few sessions with Ron I started to shoot reasonably well and, with plenty of practice, I continued to improve. In 1997 I bought a Berretta 20 bore – much easier to handle than a 12 bore – after Mark pointed out to me that I was not as strong as I had been when younger. Andrew Cowie persuaded me to return to Harrogate although by now Ron had died and the shooting school had been taken over by his son Ian. Ian was quite a different character from his ebullient father but, nevertheless, a very effective teacher. I am now into my first season since my time spent with Ian and things seem to be working out very well, although I am not yet as steady as I was with a 12 bore. There are, however, the occasional flashes of genius, akin to an 18 handicap golfer getting a birdie on the 18th hole!

We have always had a spaniel and a border terrier in the house, the spaniel working as my gun dog. Shooting with a good gun dog gives so much pleasure. My favourite was Jason, who was not a huge dog, but strong and with the heart of a lion. He was an excellent hunter. In the early 1990s Jason died of a brain tumour, and we never replaced him. Mark has two spaniel bitches and one of them, Hattie, is Jason's daughter. Hattie is now nine and I occasionally borrow her for days on the grouse moor.

I have shot at various locations throughout the North East, particularly at Wolsingham where I have shot for the past 30 years with Tom Fenwick. Tom's wife Sally is always an excellent hostess, and puts up with my muddy sticks all over her house with very good grace. It is a family shoot with some guest guns: Tom and his sons James and Jolyon, Sandy Dickinson, Ken Steel, Geoffrey Barkes, Edmund Luxmoore (who died recently) and latterly Roger Booth, who was in Evans House with me at Sedbergh. In good grouse years (not that many, of late) we would have an afternoon shooting grouse after a morning with pheasants – one of the greatest shooting combinations I know.

I have also shot at Harehope on the Wrangham estate for over 30 years, at first with John Baxter (who ran the Mini Harehope shoot), Keith Tate and others. Zan Baxter, Sally Tate and Sue were the mainstay of our beaters in those early days. I then moved on to Big Harehope with John Baxter, Whaley Heppell and the estate owner himself, Ted Wrangham. These days only Ted remains, the other two both having died, and I now shoot with him and his son John, who farms the estate. Anne, Ted's wife, picks up with the aid of Dash (who had an affair with Jason) and Bo (the outcome of Jason and Dash's union). Ali, John's wife, kindly provides lunch for me and my guest. We have all had great fun over the years. I recall one day in Mini Harehope in particular. We had risen extremely early to shoot the morning duck fight. John and Keith and I went up to the moor ponds with Willie Smailes, the head keeper, shot seventeen duck and two geese, then came down from the moor and repaired to the pub at Chatton for porridge and bacon and eggs. We were joined by Mike Pyman, who had failed to get out of bed early enough to go duck shooting with us. In the two hours after breakfast the four of us then proceeded to shoot eight pheasant, one woodcock, one partridge and a pigeon before meeting our wives on the moor for a picnic lunch. They then beat two mini grouse drives for us and we shot two brace of grouse and a snipe. A truly memorable day!

I shot for eight years on the Joicey estate, at Millfield and Flodden with Ian Fraser, Andrew Cowie, Bill Capper, Colin Herbert and Jonathan Hayward among others. This was a truly splendid shoot with a lot of dramatic drives, such as the Black Wood. As with all good things, it had to come to an end, but I still have some very exciting memories.

In the 1970s Derek Knowles bought Winnows Hill, a small hill farm near Blanchland which boasts an excellent duck pond, hill partridge, grouse and wild pheasant. Some of my most memorable shooting days have been spent at Winnows Hill. I recall shooting with Derek and Michael Joicey one day in November. We had a marvellous mixed bag of about forty head. The high point of the day was a picnic on the hill in warm, brilliant sunshine. Grouse shooting was quite easy for me there, but not so easy in other places, such as Hepple or Williamston where some areas remained inaccessible, except in a very dry year. However, I have had some lovely days on those moors with Peter Vaughan and Stanley Gill. I also treasure the days when Tom Cowie invites me to shoot at Holwick and Wemmergill, generally accompanied by Mark who drives me about and looks after me.

In the 1980s Mark and I started running a charity clay pigeon shoot with the generous help of Jack Reed at his shooting grounds near Dinnington, on May Day, the old communist Bank Holiday. These were enormous fun and raised surprisingly large amounts of money which went to Disability North for the first ten years or so but which in recent years has gone to the Julie Kent Trust, a small local charity for Cystic Fybrosis.

Over the years I have also been privileged to visit many fine pheasant shoots in north Northumberland as a guest – among them Ford and Etal, Roddam, Duddo, Westnewton, East Learmouth and Middleton Hall.

One hobby that I have been able to enjoy all my life is painting in water colours. My daughter Nicola has far more talent than me, but I maintain that she must have got it from somewhere! It is generally when we are on holiday that I feel the urge to paint, probably because it is at these times that I am fairly relaxed and time is not at a premium. One advantage of water colour as a medium is that you have to work fast with most subjects – the object is to create something fresh and sparkling and it is no good throwing too much paint at it, or going over it again and again, because it would then lose its immediacy and freshness. Consequently, unless you are painting something which requires an intricate drawing (for example, a cathedral) you should finish a painting inside an hour or two at the most.

Paper is very important and I have gradually increased the strength and thickness of the paper that I use over the years, now using, for preference, a 300lb (per ream) paper rather than anything lighter. I also tend to favour rough, rather than smooth. I don't use a lot of colours, but try to avoid greens and use ochres, deep reds and blues which somehow seem to suit watercolours rather better. Alarizon crimson makes some lovely colours when mixed with blues. I have experimented with hake brushes as advised by Ron Ranson but cannot get away with them, and favour instead a more conventional, largish brush which gives a broad wash which I can control. Painting is a very subjective artform, and rules make a poor substitute for experienced intuition and flair. I have never exhibited, except at charity art shows such as those that Disability North mounts every year. If any of my pictures are sold I give the proceeds to the charity. My enjoyment from this hobby is intensely personal and individual: I have lost count of the number of paintings that have been torn up before I have produced a finished article that meets with my satisfaction.

Sue's sister Jane is a professional artist and a leading expert on silk painting and I have valued her advice over the years. Nicola is also a professional, so my work has to stand considerable family scrutiny and good-humoured banter.

In 1972, I was introduced to the Wranglers Debating Society by Maurice Lowther. I remember that Hugh Speed and Ken West joined the Society at the same time. Once I had survived the first few years of critical examination by the older members, I thoroughly enjoyed the test of leading in a debate and the cut and thrust of seconding or speaking from the floor. The most important speeches in a formal debate are the leaders' summing up and I have seen many a result swing on the strength of these closing speeches.

The Wranglers Society is nearly one hundred years old and is one of three debating societies in Newcastle founded around the turn of the century. The other two are The Lithosians and the Junior Lithosians. Tradition plays a considerable part in debating ritual and extreme courtesy is extended by members to each other, particularly when they are meta-phorically stabbing one another in the back during a debate. The business meeting which precedes the debate is a battleground of ancient ritual and the objective of the chairman is to conclude the meeting at the time appointed for the start of the debate. The objective of the members is to cause as many interruptions to the chairman's smooth path as possible so as to defer the start of the debate by up to – or even, occasionally, exceeding – half an hour. The Society traditionally meets for several debates in the winter months and I recollect in the 1970s being instru-mental in moving The Wranglers' home to the Northern Counties Club where it has happily debated for this last twenty years. A high point is the Pot Pie Supper which takes place shortly before Christmas, where members are given unprepared subjects on which to speak and the re-mains of the cheese (by tradition a half Stilton) are given to the Wrangler who performs the best. I never won the cheese.

The debating season concludes with a Dinner in March which has been held in the County Hotel for as long as I have been a member, with considerable ceremony and panache. The printed menu extends to eight pages and is studded with quotations illustrating the faults and virtues of the members and their decisions. Each Wrangler takes it in turn to propose the Abstract Toast: after one hundred years the choice of subject is somewhat limited. He also takes his turn at replying to the Toast, pro-posing toasts to the Guests and to the Chairman, acting as Chairman of the Dinner and, most industrious of all, acting as Secretary to the Society.

––––––

For thousands of years mankind has enjoyed wine. Even the Bible (Ec-clesiastes) encourages us to "drink thy wine with a merry heart". I have never attempted to do anything different and wine has always given me much pleasure. Travelling throughout the world gives one a great oppor-tunity to taste wine in its country of origin and my experience is that the cheap wines taste infinitely better drunk fresh, in their birthplace, than when they have been brought back to England, which often proves not to be a harmonious environment. For example, Greek wines can be delicious in Greece but are particularly bad travellers and seem out of place in our cold climate.

I have been lucky to have visited South Africa, the Napa Valley of California, New Zealand and Australia and tasted a lot of "colonial" wine. It is mostly very good and it is heartening to see how standard of vini-culture have developed over the last 20–30 years. I have drunk and enjoyed wine all over the Mediterranean but my wine heart is in France. Sue and I have spent some memorable times visiting vineyards all over France. Perhaps the most interesting was with David Lowry, when we arrived by appointment one morning at 9.00 am at Riquewihr, the little fortified town on the Alsace wine trail, to meet Jean Hugel, the head of the famous family firm which had just celebrated 350 years of wine-making! Jean gave us a whole morning and although we visited the cellars and tasted some wine, most of the time was spent talking and drinking coffee and listening to his wonderful stories about the great family business. They had marked their recent anniversary by inviting 350 guests from all over the world's wine trade, and between them they drank one thousand bottles of wine. Alsace wine is curiously more additive-free than most other wines and thus it is quite difficult to get a hangover when drinking Alsace wine.

Sue and I both love dry white wine made from the Sauvignon grape and we sometimes spend time in France tasting in vineyards as far apart as Sancerre on the Loire to the South West, where many new wines are being made, sometimes by 'foreigners'. Unlike Sue, I love white burgundy and we have also spent some time exploring the Burgundy region. I remember one day near Rully, where I spent the morning painting a chateau, whilst Sue went for a walk. Then we called in at a farmhouse where a *degustation* was taking place. Outside was a tandem bicycle and a rather grand Rolls Royce. The gloom inside made it difficult to see, but we were warmly welcomed by *Madame*, who sent her son scurrying off to find us glasses and some wine to taste. *Monsieur* was enjoying himself hugely and had obviously been tasting his own wine to excess, for he was paralytic! The Rolls belonged to a fat Parisian and the tandem to a charming young couple from Denmark, who explained that they had a camper van in the next village, in which they would return later to collect the wine they had bought, but that they were cycling for fun and exercise. They reckoned to stock up with a year's supply from their French holiday.

I like most wine, and particularly red burgundy, claret and good Rhône wine. One of the objects of wine tasting in France – and in England – is to keep my cellar topped up with good wine. I am a member of the Wine Society, enjoy its literature and acknowledge that it has taught me a lot. I use several other wine merchants, particularly Andrew Mead, who used to be a schoolmaster and whose hobby (wine) eventually became his profession; Richard Granger, whose cellars at West Jesmond Station are conveniently close and whose house wine is called "Chateau de la Gare"; and Gordon Armstrong who supplies me with the most excellent and very reasonable house champagne.

Of all our many sorties throughout France one of the most rewarding was a visit to Madiran, a little known wine region fairly near the Pyrennees. Madiran produces a very strong red wine which, by law, must be kept in the barrel for three years. It is the prettiest and most delightful place, which affords occasional glimpses of snow-clad mountain peaks in the distance illuminating the view. One morning we found ourselves beside a very pretty château, the Château de Peyrus, and asked an old lady who was sweeping leaves from the drive near the lodge gates whether we might taste some of the local wine. She turned out to be the lady of the house, and invited us in to her kitchen where we were privileged to taste a most delicious red wine. I bought a few bottles, which improved very well with age. The lady was English, and had married the French owner of the chateau before World War II. During the war, when the Germans arrived, they lived in the woods and were part of the Resistance. They now had many grandchildren, some of whom had been brought up in France, some in England. She directed us to the village of Madiran where we had a wonderful – and very cheap – lunch.

My own modest cellar is a reflection of my love of wine. It reminds me of France and all the other wine producing regions of the world that I have been lucky enough to have visited over the years. Luckily, too, I am still able to descend the small staircase and keep my cellar in reasonable order.

In the last twenty years Sue and I have discovered the great pleasure that can be derived from exploring the back roads of France and it is a joy to drive on quiet roads once one has crossed the Channel, after slogging round our crowded island with its lethal motorways. For a disabled person, the car has a number of advantages as a means of holiday transport. It gives one the freedom to depart from home when you want to, rather than being at the mercy of a train timetable or airport departure times, or package tour restrictions. It is easy to fit in to the car everything that you want to take, and equally bring home everything that has caught your fancy. It also gives you the freedom to roam; to stop for lunch where you please and spend the night where you want (although personally I would rather book ahead so that I can be assured of a good night's rest). Planning is all part of the pleasure of a French holiday. The Hovercraft is also a very convenient means of crossing the Channel for a disabled person. Because it can only carry a limited number of vehicles (about 30-40 cars) you can park quite close to the passenger area for the crossing and there are only three steps to negotiate into the hovercraft, with a good handrail. The terminal building is also small, and within easy walking distance for me on my crutches are the Bureau de Change, the Duty Free Shop, the disabled loo and a cup of coffee. The best aid to the planning of a French holiday in recent years has been the publication of Gayot's *France*, with the best of *Gault Millau Guide France,* which has an account (in English) of more than 700 frank and witty reviews of restaurants, hotels and the countryside. Over the years we have explored many lovely backwaters, but France is a big country and I know that there are plenty of places still remaining for us to discover.

The magnetism of Constantine Bay in North Cornwall has never faded, and we have been returning there for holidays for over forty years. Originally we shared Lees Nook with the Sadlers. Lee was a wrecker, a popular Cornish sport in the old days and the cottage is conveniently situated next to some very sharp, rocky cliffs as well as a glorious surfing beach. As time went by and the children grew up, we grew too big for the cottage, which belonged to the local doctor's family. They also owned a field at the back of the dunes in which they conveniently built two chalets – one for the Sadlers and one for us! Eventually the Sadlers built their own house nearby, but we still re-visit the chalet which has been rebuilt in the more recent past. What is the attraction of Constantine Bay? First, the surfing, which is quite challenging and is now supervised by lifeguards; second the golf – Trevose Golf Club is owned by Peter Gammon and is a splendid seaside links. When I was fit I enjoyed many a fine match with Peter when we both played off six handicap and I enjoyed accompanying Mark around the course in a golf buggy a few years ago. There are great views up and down the coast which make Constantine Bay and the surrounding area a good place to paint which, for me, partially makes up for not being able to surf or play golf. I have always been warmly welcomed in the Clubhouse bar and the beer tastes as good as ever. We always seem to see a few old friends when we are down, particularly the Venner family from Birmingham. Padstow is the epitome of a romantic Cornish fishing port and Rick Stein's fish restaurant has added a touch of glamour in recent years.

Going further afield normally means taking a flight and Newcastle now has quite a number of direct flights to holiday venues such as the Mediterranean. We were able to take advantage of this facility to enjoy a once-in-a-lifetime family holiday in Majorca in 1996, which I describe in the following chapter.

A holiday in the sun for one or two weeks can be enjoyable and invigorating but the hassle of air travel for disabled people is, in my view, getting worse. Recently we decided to abandon our plans for a holiday in the Caribbean when we discovered that to travel Club Class would cost us an additional £2000 each. For two weeks in the sun we concluded that it was just not worth it.

Arthur Young was at the forefront of professional firms with its policy of allowing senior partners to take sabbaticals. I was fortunate in that the timing of my age, seniority and length of service allowed me to take two sabbaticals; the first in 1980 for three months' duration. The purpose of a sabbatical was merely to allow jaded partners to recharge their batteries and there was no compulsion on one either to study or to write. Nevertheless when Kenneth Wright, a former President of the Institute of Chartered Accountants, heard that I was entitled to a sabbatical, he suggested to me that a useful exercise for me would be to update Tom Hamilton-Baines' text book on Share Valuations, knowing of my interest in the subject. Although Kenneth was an executor of Tom's estate he did not realise that the publishers had given identical instructions to Michael Pitts, a senior partner of Chalmers Impey in Birmingham. I knew Michael well, because he was President of the Birmingham Society at the same time that I was President of the Northern Society. On learning that we had both been asked to undertake the task of updating Tom's book we decided to toss a coin; perhaps not the most common practice in the publishing world, but as a result he did the job and I was able to enjoy a sabbatical untroubled by work and with a clear conscience to boot.

Sue and I pondered how best to use this fortuitous gift of time in the mainstream of my professional life. Eventually we decided to take a villa in Corfu for a month, with me driving out through the Balkans with my son Mark and his girlfriend Debbie, and Sue, Nicola and her fiancé Chris, and Sue's mother flying out to join us. The journey out was extremely interesting but somewhat marred by the fact that Mark was unwell, which meant that none of us enjoyed it as much as we might have done. The villa was called 'Olive Trees'. The eponymous trees grew in the centre of the patio, providing a natural stage upon which most of the action was played out: breakfast, coffee, games of mah-jong, scrabble, and dinner if we were there. We hired a boat for two weeks and made frequent mini-voyages around the coast opposite Albania, calling at one of the numerous tavernas along the Corfu coast for lunch. We joyfully explored Corfu's many treasures by both car and boat and the month slipped by in a flash. Sue's mother's place was taken by Sue's niece, Lisa Venables, after a fortnight, which provided an excuse to visit Corfu town and see the cricket match in the main square. We were all sorry when the time came to leave and Sue, Nicola and I took the car to the docks to get the ferry to Brindisi on the heel of Italy. The next three weeks were spent driving up through Italy and France, during which we added vastly to our knowledge of European culture, discovering many gems along the way which we have re-visited since. One such was the village of Lamastre in the Auvergne. A place that time seems to have forgotten, the cuisine of its Hôtel du Midi shines as a star even amongst the wealth of culinary splendour that bejewels *la belle France*.

I still had time to fit in a few days' fishing in Scotland after getting home before I had to return to the office.

Eight years later, Sue and I set off to explore the Far East. On this occasion the constraints of time meant that our visit was kept to nine weeks, but we managed a month in New Zealand and a week each in Sydney, Lizard Island, Singapore, Penang and Bangkok. The absence of traffic in South Island, New Zealand is quite remarkable. It is possible to drive for an hour without passing a car and the other amazing thing is that you can experience every sort of weather within the space of one day, travelling east to west. Hot sun on the Canterbury Plain, cold rain in the foothills, snow blizzards crossing Arthur's Pass and then the warm tropical rainforests of the west coast. We spent most of our time in South Island staying with friends of friends at sheep stations and the hospitality was tremendous. On one occasion a two year old Merino sheep was killed in our honour – it was as tender as young lamb and much tastier! That particular station was over 100,000 acres and the Merinos lived all year in the mountains being brought in once a year to be sheared. On another occasion we went up into the hills in an old Land Cruiser, driving on tracks that were, to say the least, hair-raising. We delivered mail and papers to a deserted farmstead that was situated in a Shangri-La type valley. We were invited in for coffee, after which we climbed higher still, well up into the mountains, to fish for rainbow trout on the edge of a large lake. I had been given a local fly called a "Mrs Simpson" and, full of anticipation, I put it on a 6lb cast and started fishing with my little seven-piece extending Hardy smuggler. As I retrieved the first cast I spotted a huge fish following my fly. My second cast was further out and I brought it back more slowly. The fish again followed the fly but did not take it. However, on the third cast, I pulled back very slowly, jiggling the fly slightly. With one tremendous dart, the fish took the fly. After an exciting fight I landed a six and a half pound rainbow. This was an enormous thrill, and our hostess cooked it for dinner that night.

We loved New Zealand, although we had not had much luck with the weather, catching our first glimpse of Mt Cook from the aeroplane which took us to Sydney from Christchurch. We were upgraded to first class on this flight and had a very exciting time rushing from one side of the deserted first class saloon to the other, as we flew over the New Zealand mountains. We were welcomed in Sydney by Anthea Marchbank, who showed us around her home town with great pride. What a beautiful city! But the best of Australia was still to come ...

We flew to Cairns and from there embarked in a very small old mono-plane with a fuselage that appeared to be held together with strapping. Our one hour flight took us up the Barrier Reef before we landed on Lizard Island which is right up in the north and was first discovered by Captain Cook when he was trapped inside the Reef. He climbed the island's highest peak (now known as "Cook's Look") which is 1002 feet high, and from there could see his escape route – a very narrow stretch through the Reef now known as "Cook's Passage". Sue followed in the explorer's footsteps up Mt Cook and earned a champagne breakfast at the hotel. Lizard Island is the closest either of us has ever been to finding our own Shangri-La. Surrounded by the most breathtaking underwater world that the great Barrier Reef has to offer, the island boasts only one small hotel and a tiny research station. When you take a boat out for a day, it is highly unlikely that you will meet anyone else.

Our next stop was Singapore, which was exciting and remarkably clean; Penang, on the coast of Malaysia, was incredibly hot but we were able to bathe several times a day. While there we bumped into Ian and Anne MacNeil: Ian was another of my 'chain gang' of past Presidents. They were exploring Malaysia by bus. Bangkok was hotter still, and busy and chaotic, its tuk-tuks filling the air with noise and dust; but we enjoyed dining by the river with its floating markets and the contrasting peace and quiet. On one occasion we went upstream for about 50 miles to the old palace where what we had taken to be a huge herd of elephants turned out to be the most magnificent topiary we had ever seen. Another day was spent visiting the Rose Gardens, about 30 miles west of the city, where we watched a splendid spectacle of Thai dancing. Sue noticed that there was a wheelchair on the other side of the stage and when we worked our way round there we found that its occupant was Sue Masham, who was travelling with her husband. It was the first time we had seen another wheelchair in Asia!

The night before our departure home was spent dining at a restaurant which is described in The Guinness Book of Records as the world's largest. It consists of a series of pagodas linked by passageways, through which the waiters brought food on rollerskates. The menu was forty pages long, at the back of which the wine list consisted of three bottles, all Australian. The pagodas all looked out across a reasonably large lake where giant carp cruised hoping for leftovers, in the centre of which was a stage for the inevitable performance of Thai dancing. A fitting end to a truly memorable holiday.

I have been very lucky to have visited many wonderful and unusual places throughout the world. Had I not had my accident I may well have travelled to a few rather more inaccessible places, but on the whole I am content to have seen and experienced all that I have done. I am firmly of the belief that it is necessary for anyone trying to lead a full and meaningful life to have both particular interests and holidays and I am most fortunate that I am able to enjoy these to the extent that I still do. Golf is, perhaps, the one game that I would still be playing if I had not had the accident, although with everything that I now do I am not sure that I could fit it in!

12

The Family

*All values are relative, but some relatives
are better value than others.*
Lord Vinson

UE AND I WERE VERY FORTUNATE in that we both managed to get on extremely well with one another's families. There were no 'mother-in-law' hang-ups, and we all became a very well-knit family group. Both my father and my father-in-law played golf at the Northumberland Golf Club, as I did, and we all met fairly regularly. We regularly visited both parents' homes for meals and also patronised the Golf Club with our parents, especially as the children grew older. We all believed that learning "golf club manners" was an intrinsic part of growing up.

We were all quite keen on celebrating anniversaries. Sue and I celebrated our tenth wedding anniversary with a fancy dress party at Northern Rugby Club. We asked our guests to dress in the costumes of the 1920s, and some quite amazing clothes were extricated from various trunks for the occasion. In 1980 my parents celebrated their Golden Wedding, and we decided to set up a marquee in our garden and give them a dinner party for 100 people, asking them to draw up their own guest list. I had laid down some champagne in anticipation of the occasion, which succeeded beyond my wildest dreams. Sue's catering business was running very smoothly by then, and she prepared the entire meal which was served by her splendidly professional and loyal team of waitresses. The marquee had to embrace two round flower beds and fitted diagonally into the garden. The ornamental cabbages in these flower beds added their own particular aroma to that of the food. The whole thing was such a success that we decided to repeat the same format the following year, only this time we kept the marquee up for rather longer.

Nicola had met Chris Maughan at Art College (CATs) and shared with him considerable artistic talent. They married in 1981 when they had both finished College and were working, Chris making sophisticated puppet models for television and Nicola illustrating books, for Penguin among others. I helped them to buy their first home, a small but charming terraced house in Cambridge.

The first event in the marquee was the wedding reception for Nicola's marriage to Chris, which was held on a lovely September day. The wedding ceremony itself had been slightly fraught because the white Rolls Royce that had been ordered to take Nicola and myself to the church never arrived. One of the neighbours stepped in to the breach and we fitted Nicola, complete with voluminous dress, into the back of a Mini. However, all other aspects of the day went without a hitch, and when the time came for bride and groom to leave the party my brother-in-law (a naval officer) stopped all traffic as Nicola and Chris weaved their way down Graham Park Road on a tandem. The party itself went on late into the night, with a very noisy jazz band and much dancing and merriment. A few days later, Sue hosted a party for the Beagles and then, on the following Saturday, we celebrated our own Silver Wedding. On this occasion we asked our guests to wear 1930s rig, and the same jazz band returned to play some very popular music from those days. I recollect that Peter Taylor (later to become Lord Chief Justice) who lived down the road appeared as a magnificent Mr Chamberlain and Richard Lewin Smith a larger-than-life King Farouk. Alas, that evening the weather failed us. Torrential rain and gales made the tent shake alarmingly as we went round in the middle of the night tightening the guy ropes.

We always made a point of celebrating Christmas in style. My parents had always dined on Christmas night, formally, in black tie. We kept up this tradition but after Sue and I returned from Malta the whole family dined at Brandling Park – her parents' home – because it was much larger. Eventually, when Mark was born and we had two children at home we started having Christmas dinner at our house in Rectory Terrace then in Graham Park Road. Once we had moved to Graham Park Road we started the tradition of holding open house after church on Christmas morning for any of our friends in the neighbourhood.

It was about a year before my accident when Sue's father lost his battle with emphysema. He was only 63 and due to retire shortly, and was, sadly, the first of our parents to die. He was an extremely popular member of the family and it was a severe blow for us all. I missed him a lot and cherished the memories of our fishing together – he had taught me so much. Sue and I helped her mother with various business decisions and she moved out of the large Practice home in Jesmond to a small bungalow in Gosforth, where she soon became established in ferrying her 'old people' to the Day Centre, several of whom were much younger than she

With the family at Buckingham Palace after receiving the O.B.E.

was! From that time on she would always come to stay with us over the Christmas holiday. My own father lived until he was 80 – about another fifteen years. In a way it was more difficult for my mother to adjust after his death because by then she was 82 and had relied heavily on him. I did what I could to comfort her and of course looked after all her business affairs.

Sue's sister Jane married Roger Venables, a naval officer who had a distinguished career in submarines. Although they bought a house in the village of Stoughton near Chichester, they spent many years following Roger's appointments around the world. It became a tradition for us to visit them at Easter (although initially they had travelled north to spend the holiday with us) and for them to visit us at New Year. I can recollect some very happy Easter weekends in Drenagh in Northern Ireland, and in Suffolk. We lived a long way apart and it was very good to see them for a long weekend. They had three children who got on very well with their north country cousins. Jane is a brilliant artist and has recently written a book on silk painting, widely accepted as a standard text on the subject. I have learnt a lot from her and suspect that perhaps Nicola has inherited some of her talent.

I had no brothers or sisters, but my relationship with my cousin Robin remained very much that of a brother. We still correspond regularly and see each other and our families fairly regularly. The deaths of our mothers touched both of us deeply.

On leaving Sedbergh, Mark spent three years at Catering College and after an adventurous and arduous long safari in Africa settled into the food trade, learning how to be a first class chef at the Box Tree in Ilkley and then learning other aspects of the trade before starting his own business making pâté in a small factory which I helped him to buy. At one time he worked for John Hildreth from Norfolk whom we had met fishing and today they are working together again on another great food enterprise. In 1987, Mark married Maryanne Cooper, who was the niece of his godfather, Percy (my former partner). They were married in our church, Gosforth Parish Church, and the reception took place in the garden of Maryanne's parents' home, not very far away from Graham Park Road, on a very chilly but sunny day in June. Sue produced a splendid supper for the occasion.

Grandchildren began to arrive before very long, Nicola's son Ben being the first, in 1986. He was followed by his sister Alice, and then Maryanne and Mark produced Jessica, now nine, and Jack, who is now seven. It has been a great joy for Sue and I to have four grandchildren and it is also

Maryanne, Jessica, Ben, Alice, Jack and Nicola
in the garden of Graham Park Road.

most agreeable that they all seem to enjoy each other's company – perhaps in part this is because they only see each other occasionally, when the Cambridge contingent are with us.

Both Sue's mother and my own mother have now died marking the end of that generation of the family and life has never been quite the same. I suppose that we were very lucky to have both sets of parents around for a reasonable amount of time during our marriage, which provided a very stable foundation for the family.

Life goes on, however, and the grandchildren come and stay from time to time. It is always good to see them enjoying life in the open air; swimming in the North Sea, and even – with a bit of pressure – accompanying us on long walks. And despite the peremptory attractions of the television, they all still take pleasure in reading. I enjoy a game of chess with Ben and refuse to let him beat me, although I suspect his enthusiasm has waned of late. Family games of Monopoly are also very popular.

In 1996 we thought that we would have a once-in-a-lifetime's holiday and get everybody together. The first hurdle was to ensure that everyone had some free time, which proved the most problematical for Chris: by this time he was working as the senior art tutor at CATs and was only able to take very short holidays in the summer. However, we were able to fix some dates at the end of July and early August and were lucky enough to find a marvellous old manor house which had been converted to sleep ten in Majorca, situated near the mountains in the north of the island. We flew out from Newcastle and hired two cars, arriving one glorious evening at this most beautiful house set in magnificent surroundings. Within minutes we were all in the swimming pool and I shall never forget that first magical evening, as the sun set behind us in the hills. Most of our time was spent relaxing in the lovely pool, and the covered area beside it where we sat, ate and nursed our sunburn. There was very little need to go out, although the coast was only three miles away. There were various friends nearby and a good golf course within half a mile and I accompanied Mark and his friends round the course on a buggy. Mark and I went exploring and found a splendid local wine merchant in a village in the middle of the island. We stocked up well, but had to return within a week to replenish supplies!

In 1993 Sue reached the milestone of 60, and the children and I decided to celebrate this with a surprise party for her. Mark and Maryanne were living at this time quite close to the church in Gosforth, and invited us to go round after church (parish communion at 10.00), where Mark cracked open a bottle of champagne. Our departure from their house, at about midday, was Mark's cue to telephone Nicola who was in charge of operations at Graham Park Road, where guests were assembling. They had all been instructed to hide their cars well away from the house so that, when Sue and I arrived home, there was no evidence at all of any activity. It was with great astonishment and delight that Sue walked into the sitting room to find it packed full of family and friends! Sue's partner Virginia had prepared a wonderful meal. More recently we have marked the passing of Sue's 65th with a lovely supper party at Rossini's restaurant in Jesmond with the whole family, including the grandchildren.

13

The Accountancy Profession

Accountancy is an inexact science.
Lord Vinson

O A VERY GREAT EXTENT the accountancy profession is self-regulating. There are a number of professional bodies, but the foremost and largest of these is the Institute of Chartered Accountants in England and Wales. This sets the qualifying examinations for its students. All members of the Institute pay a subscription to support an organisation which presides over the affairs of the profession, takes a lead in training both before and post-qualifying, and disciplines its members. Throughout the country, members are supported by District Societies of the Institute and the accountancy students are supported by Students Societies which mirror the relevant District Societies. It is expected that members should give a proportion of their time to support the profession and thus the officers of the District Societies are made up of professional accountants in practice or in industry.

In common with my fellow students I took part in the affairs of my Students Society when I was a student and in the ensuing years I attended many courses run by the Institute at Cambridge and by the Northern Society at Otterburn in Northumberland and elsewhere, and eventually took my turn at lecturing on the Institute's courses on Inflationary Accounting.

I was elected to the Northern Society Committee in 1973 and in due course became Chairman of the Courses Committee. Training was assuming a bigger role in the affairs of the profession as we strove to improve our standards and match the expectations of our clients. The Northern Society Courses Committee found that they were running quite a big business. Gradually I became more involved with Northern Society and Institute affairs leading to my year as President of the Northern Society in 1979/80. The Northern Society by this time had nearly 3000 members and I was proud to be elected their President There was a great spirit of comradeship in Northern Society, perhaps partly due to regional configuration being the Northern outpost of the Institute, partly to the natural friendliness of Northerners. Whatever the reason, inter-firm rivalry was largely forgotten and partners from competing firms worked happily and effectively together for the good of the profession.

I set certain targets for my year of office, mostly to do with improving the excellent standards set by my predecessors. What was notable about my year was that it marked the centenary of the Institute and there was much celebration up and down the country, with a special conference in London attended by representatives from accounting organisations world wide. I remember meeting a very large and distinguished Nigerian in the lift at this conference who greeted me familiarly and reminded me that we had been fellow students in Newcastle. He was the Finance Minister in the Nigerian government. My fellow District Society Presidents and I were known as "The Chain Gang" and we spent a great deal of time travelling around the country, dining (probably too well) and running the business of the profession. Our wives came with us and we got to know each other extremely well, which proved to be one of the great pleasures of that year. The Institute had many problems to deal with: improved accounting standards, wondering whether to merge with other account-ancy bodies and trying to preserve our image as a fair and independent

"The Chain Gang", *HMS Belfast*, 1980. R.C.S. front row, second from left.

profession. I put a lot into that year but I also got a lot out, and I made many friends.

At the end of our presidential year, the Chain Gang dined, with our wives, on *HMS Belfast*, and this was the first of our reunions which have taken place every year since. Our leader was David Richards, who was the national President in the centenary year and who, together with his wife Stephanie, attends as many of our reunions as he can. We were quite a distinguished group, and many of the Gang served on the Council of the Institute. Two of the group – Ian McNeil and Michael Chamberlain – have since become Presidents of the Institute and John Bird has twice served as a District Society President. Sue and I look forward enormously to our annual reunion when we know we will see so many old friends. In 1984 it was my turn to organise the reunion and Sue and I, helped by Warwick and Shirley Wilson from Lancashire, took the Gang to the Lake District. We were lucky to find Underscar, a Gothic Italian mansion built in the last century above Keswick, and owned and run as a hotel by Neil Hunter who was Chairman of the House Committee of the Calvert Trust nearby. We had the place to ourselves so it was very much our own private house party, and Neil looked after us wonderfully well. The weather was glorious and we relished showing off the Lake District in ideal conditions to our friends, many of whom had never visited the area before. Someone had brought along a jigsaw of *HMS Belfast* where we had dined together at the end of our year. The jigsaw was duly set up in the hall and lasted until about 2.00 am on the Sunday morning, when a loud shout signified its completion. On the Sunday we had our own service in John Spedding's private chapel on the shore of Lake Bassenthwaite, and raised the roof with our singing.

A few years after serving as President I was asked if I would stand for the Council of the Institute to represent the Northern Society. However, it was decided that my firm had sufficient representation on the Council and we could not really afford the great amount of partner time which I would have had to give, so I reluctantly declined.

In 1991, I was astonished to be selected as the Founding Societies' Centenary Award winner. This award is bestowed upon a Member of the Institute who has made an outstanding contribution in any field of endeavour and my citation read that it was "in recognition of his outstanding contribution to the professional, economic and community life of the North East of England and for his work on behalf of the disabled and the under-privileged." The ceremony took place at a magnificent banquet at the Cutler's Hall in Sheffield (Sheffield was one of the four founding societies). Sue accompanied me and we were entertained magnificently.

Dinner at Cutler's Hall, Sheffield.

I met a lot of old friends: members of the Chain Gang, many partners from my firm from all over the country and a strong contingent from the Northern Society. I was presented with a statue of Economia, the Goddess of Accountancy, by Sir Peter Middleton, the permanent Secretary to the Treasury, who proposed the toast to me, and reproduce here the text of my reply, which reflects many of my feelings at the time:

"Mr President, Mr National President, Sir Peter, Ladies and Gentlemen:
I feel rather like the boy who wrote home to his mother from
school and said 'I want to leave because of five very good reasons. First,
I hate the work. Second, I hate the boys. Third, the boys hate me.
Fourth I hate the staff and fifth, the staff hate me.' His mother wrote
back and said, 'Don't be silly, you must stay because of two much better reasons. One, you are 47 and second, you are the headmaster.'

May I first thank Sir Peter for his most generous and up to the minute obituary, accorded to me in terms of kindness and of compliment far beyond my merits, and containing much that no man should hear till dead. As my life has unfolded in recent years I have been astounded to find honours being bestowed upon me. I have never had the advantage of a University education and yet next week someone has waved a magic wand and I am to become a Doctor of Civil Law. It is a bit like Alice in Wonderland.

The very quality and character of this distinguished assembly imposes on me an extremely difficult task. I have to walk the tightrope of acceptability between unseemly mirth on the one hand and vacuous platitudes on the other. You will no doubt be indulgent judges of how I perform.

I regard it as a very great honour to be invited to this splendid hall this evening and to see around me so many faces of old friends and comrades in my profession and to receive this statue, the replica of which I shall greatly treasure and value and which will be preserved and handed down with my most precious possessions. I am sure that Economia, the lady of serious aspect, must have a sense of humour if she is to spend the rest of her life with me.

It also gives me great pleasure to look at the list of those men who have previously received this honour and this makes me wonder, grateful though I am, why I am included among these very distinguished men. I also wonder, perhaps irreverently, if and when a woman will be chosen for this honour? Perhaps Economia might approve.

Let me begin my remarks by recalling some incidents that have happened in my experience of the profession. I start by telling you one benefit of having been given this award. I was prompted to remind myself about the history of our profession and I am indebted to that doyen of the Northern Society, Stanley Middleton, for the loan of several books. In fact, he is the author of one of them, the history of our own Northern Society. I felt I had to get this award into some sort of perspective and in so doing I observed some interesting facts. The first was that Insolvency was just as important, indeed possibly more so, to our accounting practices in 1880 as it is today. The second was that our forbears of 100 years or so ago seem to have had much better appetites for both eating and speaking than we do today. This is no criticism of your hospitality, Mr President, rather admiration for our predecessors' stamina. In those days, dinners seemed to have ten courses with six or seven different wines followed by ten or twelve speeches. The proceedings had to start at 5.30pm in order to terminate by midnight. The third thing I noticed was that relationships between London and the provinces don't seem to have changed much in 100 years.

I think that the Founding Societies were very well served by their

Presidents in the Centenary Year of the Institute, which is when this Award was inaugurated. We were all part of the same Chain Gang – and what a crew we were! Now getting rather older, they all swear blind that they did not know anything about my nomination for this award and if they had, they would have put in a black ball. Contrary to the usual custom around the country, the President of the Northern Society never speaks at his dinner. By forcing me to speak tonight this may be a way in which they are getting even.

My year as President of the Northern Society was a great highlight in my professional life and one day sticks out in my mind: when I chaired the first official function of the Institute's Centenary Year, on 10 January 1980. This was a luncheon held in Newcastle and I well remember the great speech to the Institute proposed by the legendary J M S Coates, who spoke in his 90th year for 45 minutes and received a standing ovation which lasted nearly as long. The unfortunate Kenneth Sharp had an impossible task in replying. No wonder I accused JMS of being a legend in his own lunchtime.

During my time in the profession I have forged many friendships of mutual trust and respect with my partners and my staff, with my clients and bankers and lawyers, with colleagues in other firms working on Northern Society and Institute affairs, and particularly with the rest of my Chain Gang. Perhaps one or two light-hearted memories can lighten the gloom of the darkened corridors of history. I remember once being appointed the liquidator of the University Theatre in Newcastle. When I attempted to take possession of the theatre following the creditors' meeting at which I had been appointed, I found the door barred by no less an august presence than Vanessa Redgrave, who was leading a sit-in. She kept me out of the theatre for five weeks. I finished up suing her union, Equity, because their members didn't actually drink the beer in the theatre, they just let it go bad!

Perhaps my largest liquidation was when I was appointed to the residuary body of Tyne and Wear County Council. We were rather proud of being the first residuary body to wrap up our affairs, and perhaps our most difficult task was to consume the wine stocks by our self-imposed self destruct date!

I am particularly glad to see so many of my colleagues from Ernst & Young here tonight. Geoff Norman, my OMP, must have had a difficult time rounding them up. I am also very pleased indeed to see Percy Cooper, whom I joined in partnership in 1958, helping him and my father to build up the practice. My colleagues in Ernst & Young well know my technical limitations. I have never been switched on by G.A.A.S. or G.A.A.P.S. or even S.S.A.P.S. or S.O.R.P.S. I have always felt that it is

With Sue and Economia.

better to create than to be learned. Creating, when all is said and done, is the true essence of life.

The last person I would like to refer to is my wife, who has been a tower of strength for 35 years. When I had an accident 21 years ago, which obviously was going to change our lives a fair bit, she took it in her stride and didn't give me any unnecessary sympathy – rather the reverse, in fact! But she could be a great help in professional matters. I remember once when I was President I was invited to the 50th Anniversary of the Société des Experts Comptables de Alsace Lorraine, in Nancy (twin town with Newcastle) and we landed in a tiny aircraft at Nancy to be met by my opposite number who couldn't speak a word of English. We spent the next two days with 300 French accountants and their wives who couldn't – or wouldn't – speak English. Fortunately Sue could speak French better than me, and it was amazing how after six glasses of champagne *la plume de ma tante* came flooding back.

My life in the community in the North East has given me the opportunity to indulge in my favourite pastime, which is meeting people and attempting to bend them to my way of thinking. I have been involved in many activities – fighting for different causes and being part of some very exciting achievements, but I feel very humble when I weigh my puny efforts against what has been achieved by thousands of dedicated people in their different spheres. My work in the field of disability has been kindly mentioned and I would only say that since 1981, the International Year for Disabled People, a much warmer wind has blown on behalf of disabled people, and I am proud to have added a bit of a puff here and there.

And if, like Martin Luther King, I am allowed tonight to have a dream, it is that when I leave the stage, the North East of England will be a better place for disabled people to have the same opportunities to live and work and play as able bodied people.

In accepting this award I thank you all for the compliment you have paid to me and through me, my colleagues in my firm who have supported me in my various adventures. And I thank you, Mr President, for your gracious hospitality this evening."

Donald Turner, who was the Senior Ernst & Young partner present, rose from the back of the hall and came up and presented me with a portrait of myself, which from that day has been known as the Secret Portrait, because I had been completely unaware of its existence. Apparently the artist had managed to infiltrate himself into my office and had taken a number of photographs of me, on the presumption that he was writing a magazine article, and he made what is generally regarded as an excellent portrait from the resulting photographs. I was quite overwhelmed, and murmured some words of thanks. I felt extremely humble at the end of a most memorable day.

14

Public Appointments

Let us ... dare to do our duty as we understand it.
Abraham Lincoln

VER THE YEARS FROM 1980 up until the present day I must have been on some list of "the good, the bad and the ugly" in Whitehall, because I have been invited to serve as a non-executive member or director on a variety of government owned companies or quangos. Generally, it was felt in the firm that, provided there was no conflict, it was a good thing for a senior partner to serve the country in this way and in a local context that partner would be seen as one of the natural leaders in the profession.

In 1980 I was approached by Tom Rutherford, the Chairman of North Eastern Electricity Board, asking whether I would like to join the Board. I had a couple of chats with him to explore what would be involved and intimated that I would like to do it. Quite some time passed before I was called to London for an interview with the Minister of Energy, then Mr Lamont. I made clear that I had no expertise in electricity but he assured me that he merely wanted a senior accountant with my sort of broad experience on the Board, and so I joined. Jack Harmsworth was the Deputy Chairman, and I got to know Tom and Jack very well over the next eight or nine years. The Board also had an excellent Chief Accountant in Alan Groves, who later became the Finance Director when the company was privatised. The Board was rather unbalanced, with only two full-time directors and seven non-executives, including three ladies. My fellow Board members included Diana Eccles, whom I had worked with on the Norseman Television bid, Bill Smart of Whessoe and James Holdsworth, a farmer from North Yorkshire. The area we covered was quite extensive: from the Tweed down to Harrogate and Scarborough and west as far as the Pennines. There were about 9000 employees of the company when I joined, and by the time I retired in 1989 we were down to around 5000, largely as a result of increased efficiency and the use of computers. The auditors of the Board were Ernst & Whinney and when my firm merged with Ernst & Whinney in 1989 I had to declare a conflict of interest, which forced me to resign.

Some of the main issues which we tackled were constantly trying to reduce the number of employees with various redundancy and early retirement packages, and trying to reduce other costs, for example by merging different activities, cutting down on the number of depots and regional offices, and generally saving overheads. We also made great efforts to improve sales, not just of electricity but of appliances through our chain of shops throughout the North East. In those days we had no charity budget – that was not on the agenda for a nationalised concern, but we were, I think, slowly assuming a regional champion role. For example, we took the initiative to get quite close to the Japanese companies who were showing interest in locating in the North East, and offering them specific deals with power. In this we were lucky that the Japanese held in great esteem – and even awe – the late Lord Armstrong, who built the world's first water-based power station at his home Cragside, in Rothbury in Northumberland. Cragside was one of the first houses to have electric light and I remember we were able to make great play of this when persuading the Japanese to come to our particular corner of the UK.

As a Board, and as individual Board members, we went around our parish fairly regularly and we would have Board meetings alternately at Carliol House, the headquarters in Newcastle and somewhere out in the regions. I remember the cook in Carliol House was a star, and produced the most amazing *cordon bleu* meals for us. Once a year, generally in the summer holiday season, we would visit a site of particular interest to the power industry. On one occasion we went to North Wales and examined the amazing power station at Dinorwic, where during the night, when there was plenty of surplus power, the contents of the lake were pumped up to a holding lake on the top of the mountain ready to be released if the National Grid was suffering an excess of demand. The inside of the mountain was like something out of a James Bond film. On another occasion we flew to Calais in a small aeroplane as guests of Electricité de France, who took us round their nuclear power station at Gravelines. Their object was to try and sell us their nuclear powered electricity direct. They entertained us to a seven course dinner one night, at the Hotel Clement in Ardres, which was quite magnificent. On another occasion we visited the controversial nuclear plant at Sellafield and came away with rather mixed feelings.

Over the years the composition of the non-executives of the Board changed and we seemed to lose most of our ladies. Sir Joseph Barnard who farmed in North Yorkshire, and Paul Nicholson – later to become

Sir Paul Nicholson – Chairman of Vaux Breweries, both joined us and as privatisation loomed on the horizon, Tom Rutherford handed over the Chair to David Morris and a new Chief Executive, Tony Hadfield, was appointed. Paul was the only non-executive to survive the changeover to the private sector although David did ask me if I would like to remain on the Board. However, the Ernst & Young conflict made this impossible. Northern Electric now started the beginnings of a Community Budget and the spirit which this engendered enabled me in 1993 to hand over the Chair of the North East Percent Club, which I had started, to David and the Chair of Business in the Community to Tony. After I left the Board I was asked to serve with Joe Barnard on the Community Affairs Panel, Joe representing the south and me the north of the region and the company developed a major community funding resource to play its part as a leading company in the private sector in the North East. Joe and I were in at the beginning and helped to shape policy. The priorities of the company had to come first and such things as branding sponsorship, for example the Northern Electric Arts Awards, were clearly most relevant. The main thing was that the regional responsibility was recognised and separate sums were set aside for sponsorship and charitable donations. We also did some secondments and tried to ensure a spread of benefits throughout the region. We selected flagship projects, and always tried to ensure that matching funding arose from our initiatives. We looked out for partnership projects and the work that Northern Electric has done over the last five or six years is generally regarded as an example of good practice in the region. More latterly the staff has set up its own charities committee and we are now seeing projects that are staff led. Overall, priorities are to try and improve the quality of life of the citizens of the North East and to add amenity value. Northern Electric has also supported the Foundations which have been set up in recent years in the region: Tyne & Wear, the Northumberland Fund (which is administered by Tyne & Wear), Cleveland, and County Durham.

One day, in the summer of 1985, I was rung up on my car phone, whilst on holiday in Cornwall, by Mr Waldegrave, then Minister of State for the Environment, who asked me if I would be prepared to serve as one of his appointees on the Northumberland National Parks Committee. This Committee was, technically, a sub-committee of Northumberland County Council, with the addition of eight or nine Secretary of State appointees and an appointee from Alnwick and Berwick District Councils.

This was something that interested me very much and I readily agreed to the request. The meetings were held in the new County Hall at Morpeth but there were quite often site visits and tours of interest throughout the National Park, which embraced a large part of the beautiful Northumberland fells. Additionally, this Committee looked after several Country Parks along the River Tyne and the North Sea Coast. The Committee was a Planning Authority in the National Park and handled a fair number of planning applications. This was the first time I had ever done any work in this field but I am naturally a countryman with my various interests in the countryside, and the work was most enjoyable.

I was the only disabled person on the Committee and I tried to further the lot of disabled people in the National and Country Parks. For example, I suggested that we make part of the Pennine Way accessible for wheelchairs and I am very glad that after my time on the Committee this has now been achieved. The Chairman, throughout my time, was Eddie Teasdale, a veteran Labour man and a thoroughly good sort. Nigel Vinson also served as a Secretary of State appointee at the same time as myself. My great friend John Baxter had been the leader of the Conservative group on the County Council and had served on the National Parks Committee before me. He told me what tremendous fun it was and how unpolitical it was. This was certainly the case when I joined the Committee, but it slowly grew more political as Labour strengthened its grip on the County Council and the Liberal Democrats started to become an increasing power. Eventually it got to the stage of pre-meetings of the different groups, which I felt was totally against the spirit of having Secretary of State appointees on the Committee and when we (the Secretary of State appointees) started meeting in a pub before the Committee meetings, I resigned.

Although I regretted having to make my decision, because I had thoroughly enjoyed serving on the Committee, I felt that politics should have been kept out of it. There were a lot of very good people on all sides of the Committee, but all too often certain members felt it necessary to turn what should have been a rational debate about a planning or priority problem into a political statement. I felt that the Committee's work was becoming less useful.

Also in 1985 I was invited to become a member of the Tyne & Wear Residuary Body. This followed the dismantling of the Metropolitan Borough Council of the County of Tyne and Wear, and it represented the biggest liquidation of my life. Our Chairman was Jock Robertson, a most interesting and extremely competent man who had spent most of his life running the Water Company in Hong Kong and who had just finished being the first Chief Executive of the Northumbria Water Authority. He had lived locally for several years and, although he had just retired to Sussex, he came up every week to run the affairs of the Residuary Body. Among the non-executive members were Stuart Sisterson, the senior partner of the leading estate agents, Storey Sons & Parker and Harry Foulkes, a former chief executive of Northumberland County Council. Our task, as in a liquidation, was to complete the contracts of the previous County Council which were still running or to negotiate a way out of them; to deal with the employees; to dispose of all the assets and to agree and settle all the liabilities. There were over 15000 employees but many of them went to the newly-formed Northumbria Police Authority and the Tyne & Wear Fire Authority. We found jobs for the rest, in the main, in the five Borough Councils that took over the five districts in Tyne & Wear, and to other Local Authorities in the region. But many found jobs for themselves. In fact, we had some considerable difficulty in keeping enough staff to finish the job.

Property was destined to be our biggest problem. There were over two thousand parcels of land or property in the estate. The most important building was the headquarters building of the County Council in Sandyford Road, which was twelve stories high and proved quite difficult to get rid of, since at the time there was a surfeit of office accommodation available in Newcastle. I can recollect that we lunched occasionally in the elegant boardroom on the penthouse floor, with splendid views overlooking the city and the river, and across to Gateshead. Among the assets that we inherited was a well-stocked wine cellar. In spite of the efforts of the County Council to reduce it before they ceased to exist, and our puny efforts during our three year term of office, there was quite a lot to be auctioned in the end. We were quite proud to be the first of the Residuary Bodies in the country to finish the task. We successfully disposed of all the assets without ever being in the position of having to give effective notice to any of the employees, and we were also able to provide the ratepayers of Tyne and Wear with a refund on their rates.

In 1990, several changes were taking place in the National Health Service and I met Sir Bernard Tomlinson, the then Chairman of the Northern Regional Health Authority, at a party one day. He told me that he was looking for non-executive directors for the Regional Health Authority, other Health Authorities and similar bodies. I told him that I would be most interested in sitting on the Regional Health Authority and in due course my appointment was made by the Secretary of State. Peter Carr, an old friend who had been the Regional Director of Employment in the North East, was made Chairman. He very kindly arranged for a disabled space to be made available for my use in the private car park, close to the front door. Among the non-executives were various old friends: Professor Mike Rawlins, from Newcastle University, who became the Chairman of the NHS's national drug committee; Tony Brown, a solicitor from South Shields, Anne Galbraith, who subsequently became the first Chairman of the RVI NHS Trust and Peter Reay from Cumbria who had been a director of Cadbury's. Subsequent appointees were Julie Flanegan of Mari, and Lady Sally Irvine, who later became my Chairman in the Newcastle NHS City Health Trust. The headquarters of the RHA were in Benfield Road which was quite convenient for me to get to. There was an enormous volume of paperwork for each meeting. Some of our work was politically sensitive and the press would surround the building at the least sniff of interesting news. Trade Unions would also surround the building to make their point during arguments about wage settlements. We dealt with extremely large sums of money, because the whole NHS budget for our region was in our charge. The region covered Northumberland, Tyne & Wear, Durham, Cleveland and Cumbria. In practice, however, most of the budget was spoken for and our debates really took place on the margins. We had various grand debates on strategy and several important ones on priorities, but following the "Health of the Nation" guidelines we attempted to re-allocate the cake for the north, with a view to making special allowances for deprived areas. I was naturally very keen on issues on disability and I was particularly keen to secure a solid future for the local spinal injury unit that was situated at Hexham. This had been built up by one dedicated orthopaedic surgeon but did not have the advantages of most of the other spinal units in the country, which were situated in or adjacent to major teaching hospitals, providing easy access to urologists and neurologists – a vital crossover for paraplegics as I knew only too well.

I recollect on one occasion representing Peter Carr at the opening of a new extension to the hospital in Kendal, which was opened by Princess Anne, and I attended innumerable seminars and strategy meetings. But it was all a bit nebulous. I found myself a very small cog in the huge NHS machine and it was difficult to place one's finger on progress. One of the things we had to deal with fairly early on was the appointment of a new

Chief Executive. We had no hesitation in appointing Liam Donaldson who is still in that position, but with an even larger remit because Northern has been merged with Yorkshire. I got on very well with Liam and also with David Flory who was our Finance Director. In the spring of 1994 my appointment to the Regional Health Authority came to an end and I was appointed to Newcastle City Health Trust, together with Sir Bernard Tomlinson, to my great delight. Peter Carr asked me if I would be Chairman but I had to decline as I was about to assume the office of High Sheriff and I could not possibly have afforded the time to do both jobs successfully. This appointment to City Health Trust dovetailed well with my work for disabled people and is dealt with in Chapter Sixteen.

15

Working For the Community

If you want to kill any idea in the world today,
get a committee working on it.
C. F. Kettering

S I GREW INTO THE SENIOR PARTNER ROLE, I started developing extramural targets for the region as a whole (in a way mirroring what happened at Northern Electric later, when it became independent). I wanted to help the industrial peace/prosperity equation and do something positive about the very poor unemployment ratios in the North East of England – worst of which was undoubtedly the Metropolitan Borough of South Tyneside.

The problems were simple in origin but complex in correction. The region had for so long depended on too few industries – coal, steel, shipbuilding and heavy engineering – and too few employers. With a drastic shrinkage in those industries a myriad alternative solutions were required to create equivalent employment for the population. One of these solutions was self-employment, but in areas like South Tyneside this was, at first, extremely difficult. Traditional employment had been the norm for generations, and in large areas of Tyneside and Wearside there was no history of entrepreneurship, which was thus regarded with suspicion. A new culture had to be created and fostered and one of the tools for this purpose was the new "Enterprise Agency". In the '80s several such agencies were established in the North East with government backing. They played a major role in developing the enterprise culture and building up the small firm sector. In Newcastle ENTRUST (The Tyne and Wear Enterprise Trust Ltd) was the leading agency with Councillor Danny Marshall as its chairman and the steady hand of John Eversley on the tiller. Although based in Newcastle, it operated throughout Tyne and Wear. In South Tyneside TEDCO (The Tyneside Economic Development Company Ltd) was chaired by Councillor Vincent Fitzpatrick, the Leader of South Tyneside Council, and managed most successfully by Tony Tomkins. Later, BEAM (Birtley Enterprise Action Management Ltd) was created in Birtley, with the help of Komatsu, and under the wing of ENTRUST, specifically to help disabled people start their own business. I joined all of these agencies as a director and I am still on the board of BEAM, which is dealt with more fully in the next chapter.

The business of an Enterprise Agency would (and still does) include training and re-training, business advice and counselling – particularly for those wanting to start a business or requiring managed workspace provision – and financial assistance and advice, and the agency would go out into the highways and byways by encouraging people to attend meetings held with the sole purpose of attracting them to self-employment. Obviously this is risky business and there have been casualties, but there has also been a phenomenal success in building up the small end of the private sector. Like other businesses, Enterprise Agencies have had to adapt to change – no longer is there automatic government funding. Their activities now have to be self-financing and they are part and parcel of a larger network helping the private sector, but they are unique in helping the most vulnerable part of that sector.

ENTRUST's chairman was supported on the board by councillors from other boroughs in Tyne and Wear, by directors of leading locally-based businesses such as Newcastle Breweries and Barclays Bank, and by senior observers from the three main government departments – Trade and Industry, Environment, and Employment (now brought together as Government Office for the North East). In the late '80s, various managed workspace projects were successfully mounted by ENTRUST, one example being the elegantly converted nineteenth century dray horse Stables belonging to Newcastle Breweries in St Thomas Street, which has seen well over 200 new jobs created. This initiative depended greatly on the leadership of David Stephenson, the Managing Director of Newcastle Breweries, and was an excellent example of a partnership between the local Enterprise Agency and a strong local business. The majority of businesses in the Stables are run by people moving into self-employment for the first time. ENTRUST therefore needed to put in place an experienced manager who could help with their day to day problems. With the Stables and various other projects safely under their belt they were ready in 1992 to tackle a bigger project, again with the help of Newcastle Breweries: converting the former St Mary's Primary School adjacent to the Breweries' main production centre in Newcastle to a Training and Enterprise Centre. Today ENTRUST handles over 20,000 enquiries for advice and assistance each year and depends on a growing band of councillors for detailed support.

The role of TEDCO was more tightly focused than that of ENTRUST, concentrating on providing premises in which people living in South

Tyneside might start up any sort of business, and then helping them with their business in its start-up phase and in its growth. Existing businesses were also helped with training, development, and marketing and they also played a role in Youth Enterprise.

From the outset South Tyneside Borough Council had the vision to see that TEDCO could provide substantial help for the borough, and Vincent Fitzpatrick was succeeded by Councillor Albert Elliott (the next Leader of the Council) as chairman of TEDCO as a mark of the Council's determination that it *should* succeed. Two very large companies, N.E.I. and Plessey, gave great support, as did many smaller companies and individuals, particularly N.E.I.'s Ron Lock, who was a tower of strength as secretary and deputy chairman, Mike Garlick, a local director of Barclays, Alan Brewster of Tyne Dock and Malcolm Sutherland of Barbour's. Plessey provided the premises for the first Business Enterprise Centre in Eldon Street and before long there was very little spare space. Some ten years later, TEDCO moved to purpose-built premises in the Viking Industrial Park. The Viking premises is now full and currently yet another new centre is being built in South Shields. TEDCO has gone from strength to strength, and is an integral part of the constant fight to help the private business sector succeed in South Tyneside and of the larger battle against unemployment.

In 1984 I was asked if I would chair the South Tyneside Industrial Strategy Committee, which was then in the process of being formed. This was a special challenge which I felt I must accept, but it was with some trepidation that I undertook the task. I was greatly helped at the start by Reay Atkinson, the regional director of the DTI, who gave me some very sound advice and a lot of encouragement. I was helped throughout by many good friends but none more so than Steve Clark, the Chief Executive of South Tyneside, who was a constant ally, helping to solve problems before they became too difficult and supporting me in every possible way. Derek Hughes, who worked for him and who chaired the working party which monitored progress, was also a tremendous support.

The Committee brought together directors and officers of the various external and internal organisations involved in the economic development of South Tyneside. Its purpose was to take an objective view of the industrial problems facing the borough and to develop a strategy designed to assist in overcoming those problems. A working party was established to develop stronger working relationships among the organisations and to prepare and implement detailed proposals to further the strategy. The need for this work had arisen from the continuing decline in the traditional industrial base and the resultant persistently high rate of unemployment. The abolition of Tyne and Wear Metropolitan County Council had left a vacuum and this made it all the more important for South Tyneside to 'get its act together'. The formation of the Committee resulted in the commitment of the necessary resources by the three major government departments as well as the various agencies and the local authority to ensure that virtually all of the actions proposed by the Committee were implemented. Initially, members of the Committee were drawn mainly from local government or central government agencies, for example Tony Pender of English Estates and Alistair Balls, regional director of the Department of the Environment. ENTRUST played a leading role as did TEDCO, but later I brought on to the Committee people from the private sector: Alan Brewster of Tyne Dock, Stan Jones from Reyrollers and Bob Tilmouth in his capacity as Managing Director of the Chamber of Commerce. Initially we defined and then set out to implement fifty nine new strategy initiatives and by 1990 we had achieved quite a lot. In 1985, unemployment in South Tyneside was nearly 30% and male unemployment was an appalling two in five. By 1990 the overall rate of unemployment had dropped to 14% – still far too high – but new employment had increased by over three thousand and unemployment had fallen by seven and a half thousand. Over three hundred thousand square feet of converted factory space had been provided; the flagship Business Park at Boldon had been established and our Tourism Initiative had led to the development of two new hotels. At a press conference in 1990 when we updated the strategy, I said:

"We have been delighted by the progress made since 1984 but we would be failing those who live and work on South Tyneside if we did not continue to pursue an energetic policy of progress, encapsulated in the new action plan which will take us on to 1995. The success of this plan depends entirely on the continued support of those councils, agencies, businesses and individuals who have joined forces to ensure South Tyneside can face the challenges of the 1990s with confidence. With that support and commitment we can achieve the enterprising goals we have set ourselves. I am confident we will succeed."

The creation of the Committee had provided an opportunity to put issues "on the map" and enabled us to force them on to an agenda at a time when there was a direct conflict between local and national political control, which was not greatly helpful. Our initiative gave it impetus, and the Committee worked extremely well together to turn South Tyneside into a success story.

Northumbria Coalition against Crime – a partnership linking the private sector with the police and local authorities – was launched in the early '90s to help the police in their battle against crime. The Coalition aimed to mobilise the elite skills and expertise of the private sector to the benefit of a wide range of crime prevention and community safety programmes and largely achieved this by setting up partnerships linking the private sector with other agencies. In 1994 I readily accepted the invitation I was given to join the board of the Coalition by virtue of my position as High Sheriff as, indeed, did my colleague the High Sheriff of Northumberland. When the Chief Constable asked Sir David Chapman (my predecessor as High Sheriff) to take on the chairmanship I told him that I would stay on the board if he would take the chair. Since then, I have chaired the Children and Young People's Committee of the Coalition. Over the last eight years the Coalition has run successful projects on auto crime, drugs education and good citizenship. My committee does both a networking job and has a pro-active role in various initiatives to keep young people from crime. I was immensely heartened when Robin Cowen, chairman of the Rank Foundation, made available some Rank money to support the work that we were trying to do. This enabled us to appoint Danny Gilchrist to head our work with young people two years ago. There is now a young team in charge of the Coalition and if I do anything at all it is to provide a few grey hairs!

The initiatives which we have led or sponsored include The Jigsaw: Young People's Vision of Utopia, involving five hundred young people throughout the region creating their visions of Utopia on 350 separate jigsaw pieces approximately one and half feet square. We worked closely with Tyneside Youth Theatre on a number of projects, one of the most innovative being a project based in a school in Sunderland and a school in Newcastle on family attitudes to rule-making and rule-breaking. We have a substantial outdoor activity programme throughout the year, including basketball and adventure training. But probably the most important initiative is the "Freshstart" programme funded by a substantial lottery bid, which makes available grants totalling £200,000 over three years to young people developing projects in the region.

In 1978 when John Walton – later to become Lord Walton – was Dean of Medicine, he persuaded me to accept the position of Honorary Treasurer of Newcastle University. I had previously served for several years as Honorary Treasurer of the University's Development Trust. The Vice Chancellor at that time was Lawrence Martin – later to be knighted – and I got on extremely well with him. Over the years I worked with many good pro Vice Chancellors particularly Jim Callaghan, John Ringrose and Richard Bailey and, of course, Duncan Murchison who became acting Vice Chancellor when Laurie Martin left. I had quite a lot to do

with the Finance Officer who for most of the time was Eric Bell, with
whom I had a very good understanding, as I did also with Derek Nicholson the Registrar. In recent years we have combined the position of
Bursar and Finance Officer and Howard Farnhill has occupied that enhanced post with considerable distinction. The Honorary Treasurer had
a number of tasks: one was to chair the Finance Committee and in the
late '70s and early '80s, although running the University's finances was
never easy, it certainly was not too dramatic. We nearly always had a
surplus due to conservative budgeting which meant that we were normally
underspent. I then had to preside over an annual auction for the surplus.
As the '80s progressed life grew tougher and I encouraged everybody to
keep our budgeting and accounting conservative. Caution was para-
mount. Instead of presiding over an auction of the surplus, I had to act
as referee to determine where savings and cuts were going to be made.
My rule of thumb was that the University's reserves should not be allowed
to drop below 5% of turnover. I hope that this helped the University get
through some of these difficult years without too much anguish but when
James Wright was appointed Vice Chancellor in 1992 he certainly had a
hard task in front of him. One of my jobs was to advise the Vice
Chancellor, but James had seen it all before at Cambridge and did not
need much advice from me. Another job the Honorary Treasurer had
was to chair the Investment Sub-committee. When I started to look at
the way in which the University's investments were managed by Lazards
I suggested that we could do with a change. We had a bidding contest
which was won fairly convincingly by Warburg's who have managed the
investments pretty well since then. After about fifteen years I handed
over to my friend David Wilson, grateful that I had had what I perceived
to be most of the 'easy' years. Ahead seemed only hard graft and a lot
of tough decisions – but I had thoroughly enjoyed my time with the
University.

In the early '80s I was dragooned by Sir Ralph Carr-Ellison into joining
the Business in the Community Tyne, Wear and Northumberland group.
The purpose of Business in the Community was to utilise the resources
mainly of locally-based, large companies in different projects which would
boost the economy and employment in the region. I have already referred
to the Stables project instigated by Newcastle Breweries; another was The
Designworks project in Gateshead, initiated by Burtons, who had a re-
dundant factory which they wished to turn to some useful purpose. The
resources of BITC were put to work and The Designworks is now home
to Newcastle's small businesses in the artistic design world. I can remember that Paddy Docherty of British Telecom was the leading light in that

very successful project. John Ward of Barclays Bank took over the chair from Ralph, and I eventually took over the chair from John before, in turn, handing it on to Tony Hadfield of Northern Electric.

One of the bright young men in my firm, Mark Hatton, worked extremely hard on different projects with me and I am very pleased that he is now a partner in the firm. One such project, which played its part in changing the lack of entrepreneurial culture, was Young Enterprise. This was generally put into schools at fifth form level and took the form of a business game, which the young people themselves would operate as a real-life enterprise. The help that they needed was mostly provided by young executives from business and the professions who would guide the youngsters as they made their decisions. One of the worst areas of Newcastle was Cruddas Park, west of the city centre, and under John Ward BITC mounted a major initiative to bring some life back to this terribly run-down estate. HRH Prince Charles had always taken a keen interest in BITC and he was a regular visitor to the Tyneside project. He came to Newcastle on another occasion, when I had been asked to chair an initial meeting of industrialists to form a Prince's Volunteers group in the North East. The idea of the volunteers was to run a training course where young unemployed people would be training alongside employed youngsters who had been released from their companies. It was hoped that in merging the two groups the unemployed would gain self-confidence and enhanced self-esteem. There has, indeed, been a very good record of employment resulting from those courses. One of the leaders of Business in the Community nationally was Sir Hector Laing (later Lord Laing), chairman of United Biscuits. In 1989 David Stephenson and I decided to set up the North East Per Cent Club, following in the footsteps of the Per Cent Clubs formed in London and Sheffield. The Per Cent Club was the inspirational arm of Business in the Community and Prince Charles lent his presence to the formation of the North East Per Cent Club in the Designworks. We achieved a membership of one hundred fairly rapidly. David was forced to take early retirement after a heart attack and I invited Ron Norman (later Sir Ron Norman) from Cleveland to join me, thus emphasising the regional nature of the Club. Prince Charles was present in spirit at our first dinner at the Civic Centre; his speech to us was relayed on to a giant video screen from some way away. Hector Laing attended the dinner, and he, too, spoke extremely well. I always tried to find inspiring speakers for the various dinners we had; on one occasion Sir Ranulph Fiennes treated us to one of his renowned and brilliantly underplayed performances. More recently Sue and I went to a dinner in the Civic Centre as guests of David Morris, the chairman of

Sir Hector Laing (later Lord Laing); David Stephenson (MD, Newcastle
Breweries) at the first dinner of the North East Per Cent Club.

Northern Electric PLC, to whom I handed the mantle when I stood down
as Chairman.

In 1988, a few us – including Nigel Sherlock, Richard Harbottle and
Carol Howells – got together with Grigor McLelland at the helm, to
establish a Foundation for Tyne and Wear. Our vision was that Newcastle,
as the regional capital, would become the centre for a Regional Community Chest which would be the leading grant-making body supporting the
voluntary sector. We were a long way behind the Americans who had
started on this course some seventy years previously.

We were challenged by the Charities Aid Foundation and the Mott
Foundation from the USA to raise one and a third million pounds to
match their two thirds of a million. Sir William Leech then raised the
stakes by another million. It was hard work but we did it, and from very
small beginnings, the Foundation grew steadily. Today it has nearly
£20 million worth of funds. I introduced my friend Sir Tom Cowie to
the Foundation and he set up his own fund under its umbrella – a fund
which is today worth £1 million. The Tyne and Wear Foundation is the
leading Foundation in the country and a great credit to everyone who

has been part of its success, particularly George Hepburn who became its first director and who, together with Grigor McLelland and Richard Harbottle, has driven it forward. I am very proud to have been a part of the process and it was with great nostalgia that we recently celebrated the Foundation's tenth anniversary.

16

Working For Disabled People

Work is much more fun than fun.
Noel Coward

LTHOUGH DISABILITY NORTH and the Calvert Trust are the two organisations to which I have given a large part of my life since my accident, I have been involved with several other initiatives concerning disability. In 1991 I was invited to join the National Advisory Council to the Secretary of State for Employment on Disabled People. Technically I was representing employers via the Association of Chambers of Commerce in the UK, but in fact the committee worked together as one to provide an independent view to the government of the day on the problems of providing and encouraging employment for disabled people. The North East was well represented. The chairman of the committee was Alan Smith, a director of Formica in North Tyneside. We also had Clive Morton of Komatsu who worked me to establish the Pinetree Centre. I chaired a working party on sheltered employment (later to be called 'supported employment') which took nearly two years and to produce its report I had great help from my colleagues, particularly Bert Massie of Radar. My other main thrust was self-employment and in this I was virtually alone on the committee. I did not – and still do not – think that the Employment Department has given sufficient priority to self-employment, but trying to make any headway on the issue was like battering against a brick wall. Again, as in other areas, I think that the North East was, and is, a leader in the field.

When one is dealing with a government body it often seems that no progress is being made. I do believe, however, that our views were taken into account and that we did have some influence on the decisions that were taken by the various ministers in charge. However, successive governments have taken a view on the level of national spending on disabled employment and without a substantial change in that view we were only able to make marginal changes.

In 1990, I joined the new Enterprise Agency which had been set up by

ENTRUST to capitalise on the initiative of Komatsu who made available the Pinetree Centre in Birtley specifically to help disabled people with employment, including self-employment. BEAM was chaired by John Eversley and it ran successfully, building up reserves primarily from the provision of workspace accommodation. At that time we were trying to ascertain the size of the self-employment problem and we were running a service with only one employee, Graham Holland, with the generally held perception that he was covering the market place. However, I was doubtful about this. Subsequent research confirmed my suspicion that there was, indeed, a large, untapped pool of disabled people who could be assisted with their endeavours in self-employment given the right circumstances and appropriate back up. It was quite clear that there would not be sufficient funds from the state to provide an adequate service, and that we would have to mount an appeal to raise funds from the private sector. By 1996 we had decided to form the Northern Pinetree Trust (which I was asked to chair) as a means of attracting tax-free charitable donations and, after some difficulty, we had our status recognised by the Charity Commissioners. The Trust's aim was to promote enterprise for disabled people.

I talked to Peter Steel, who was quite confident about the prospects of an appeal. In the summer of 1997 we had a very successful brain-storming working day during which we sorted out priorities. Shortly afterwards Mike Leathrow (who had run Komatsu after Clive Morton left) was, luckily for us, 'between jobs', having left Komatsu but not yet having taken on another assignment and thus had time to work for the Pinetree Trust to put together our development plan. With BEAM providing enough money to grease the wheels we appointed Andrew Hodson as temporary general manager. Andrew and I went to see Olivia Grant, who runs the Tyneside TEC, and she generously gave us £30,000 to kick off our appeal. Pinetree is a most exciting project which has been developing steadily for the last two or three years. I look forward to seeing it through the next two or three years, at least. It is also encouraging to note that we are not alone. Last year the Prince's Youth Business Trust launched a national campaign called "Boost", inviting me to join the Lord Mayor in Newcastle to launch the scheme there in July. It followed similar lines to the Pinetree Trust and was concerned with raising awareness about self-employment for young disabled people.

My position as non-executive director of the Regional Health Authority led directly to my appointment as a director of Newcastle City NHS Trust, where I served with Sally Irvine as chair and Lionel Joyce as the Chief Executive. I was delighted that Sir Bernard Tomlinson joined me as a non-executive together with Deborah Jenkins, Judy Hamilton and Jan Walker. Bernard was forced to retire at the age of 72 and was replaced, after a considerable gap, by Roger Vaughan, previously chairman of Swan Hunter. The role of non-executive director of City Health was substantially different from that of the Regional Authority, where we dealt solely with strategic issues. The business of City Health Trust was with mental health, rehabilitation of physically handicapped people, working with GPs in the community, non-acute child health, the health of the elderly and the installation of day surgery facilities on the General Hospital site. When we started we had a small nucleus from the old Mental Health Trust but apart from that a completely new team with, for example, a new finance director, a new medical director and a new nursing director. To help build team spirit and to help create our own strategic planning we had several 'away days' in the first two years. I found those most helpful to clear my thoughts about the direction in which we should be heading. Over the last three years we have slowly moved towards a new management style, away from the stereotypical reporting of departmental heads to Chief Executive and devolving responsiblity to clinicians via strategic programmes with sub-discipline groups.

As we have become more sophisticated in NHS contracting I believe we have been running a tighter ship, although we do not seem to be getting much benefit yet from the government's stated intent to move cash from the acute to the primary/secondary sector. Part of our thinking included the formation of task groups with therapists and specialist nurses to back up GPs. This is a new and exciting concept which deserves to succeed but it is going to be a hard road to pursue to ensure adequate funding.

I seemed to gravitate naturally towards the Audit Committee, becoming its first chairman. I developed relationships with the internal auditors and with Touche Ross our external auditors, and over the first three years of the life of the Trust we gradually got a grip on the organisation. All the non-exeuctive members of the board played a 'godfather' role over some part of the Trust, which I did for Hunters Moor Regional Rehabilitation Hospital. I was well equipped for this, having been shadow chairman for a Trust which never came into being, covering *inter alia* neurological rehabilitation. I therefore knew my way around Hunters Moor pretty well and I had a strong working relationship with Mike Barnes who had been created our first Professor of Neurological Rehabilitation.

I sat on the remuneration committee and also on an exciting future planning committee for the General Hospital site, which was looking a long way ahead to the re-building of the site. We appointed excellent architects, the Napper Partnership, and before I left we were starting to get to grips with some of the intractable problems such as car parking. Like the other non-executive members I acted as a "hospital manager", serving on appeal panels for patients who had been sectioned under the Mental Health Act. Sometimes these were very depressing, but equally some could prove extremely moving and satisfying. I chaired several appointment panels and had a strong working relationship with the finance director Sharon Barlow, and latterly with Simon Featherstone who took over when Sharon left to start a family. My appointment ceased in October 1997, and like many in other Trusts I was not reappointed. However in the middle of 1998, with my position on the Board still vacant, it appears that I may, after all, be appointed again. I hope so, because there is a lot of unfinished business to complete.

In 1991, Mike Barnes started Action for Disability, a registered charity based on Hunters Moor and asked me early on to join as a trustee. Action for Disability has an international reputation for its support for disabled people in the poorer developing countries and works closely with local partners to establish innovative, community-based rehabilitation projects in rural India. It is about to spread its experience and expertise into Tanzania through the contacts which Dr Richard Walker (a cousin of Sue's) has brought to the Trust. Recently, the first phase of a new educational project for disabled survivors of the war in Bosnia and Herzogovina was completed and the Trust has built links with the few remaining rehabilitation professionals there, to help them develop new skills for the benefit of the many disabled and disadvantaged adults and children. Back in Newcastle, Action for Disability helps to raise knowledge and awareness about disability by organising study days, workshops and courses which enable many professionals to obtain a university qualification in neurological rehabilitation. This unique venture will be expanded in 1999 to offer a residential course for people from overseas to spend six weeks in Newcastle working towards a university certificate, again offering particular knowledge about people with brain and spinal injuries. In 1996, the charity organised the first World Congress of Neurological Rehabilitation in Newcastle which attracted over 700 distinguished visitors from all over the world. It also has one of the best disability libraries in the country and works extremely closely with the Centre for Rehabilitation and Engineering Studies at Newcastle University. I am very pleased to have been able to help, in my small way, to get it established.

The outdoor sports in which I participate (fishing and shooting) are minority sports, even more so for disabled people. There are, however, several sports clubs for people with disabilities in the area, for example

Ponteland, Hexham, Wallsend and St Dunstan's Hospital. There must also be others of which I am not aware. But in relation to fishing I have been a member, since shortly after my accident, of the Westwater Angling Club which has the two reservoirs at Hallington, near Colwell in Northumberland. Over twenty years ago I persuaded the Newcastle and Gateshead Water Company (in the shape of my old friend Maurice Lowther, its chief executive) to facilitate access for disabled people by building ramps down to the lakes. These have been of tremendous benefit for wheelchair users and for elderly fishermen. On the many occasions Peter Goodison and I have fished together and I know that without those ramps it would have been virtually impossible for Peter to have got into the boat. Derek Robb is another person who comes to mind whose fishing was made much easier with the aid of the ramps. I wish more disabled people did fish, since it is one of the best ways of getting fresh air and exercise. As I have said elsewhere, once you are in a boat, your legs do not matter so much!

Peter helped me enormously to build up the Kielder Calvert Trust and when he died in 1990 he was very much missed for his enthusiasm, dedication and example. He also inspired another important activity, the Spirit of Enterprise Awards, which came into being following his death. John Bridge, chief executive of Northern Development Company, had run with Peter (and pushed his wheelchair) in the Great North Run for a few years prior to 1990. That year we set up the Spirit of Enterprise as a Trust to provide inspiration and to recognise significant business achievement by people with disabilities through a reward mechanism.

Peter had been an inspiration to everyone he came into contact with, both disabled and able bodied alike, and his achievements in the workplace in spite of physical handicap served as a great example to disabled people. He had a successful and varied career before joining ENTRUST in 1982 as their first business consultant there and he helped many new businesses establish themselves. Every year since he died a Spirit of Enterprise Award has been given to a disabled person in the North East. These Awards have generally been presented in the glare of television publicity, at first with the BBC as part of the Annual Business Awards and more recently with a special programme of our own by Tyne Tees Television. Spirit of Enterprise has been administered by Northern Development Company since its inception and today the trustees provide for an annual prize and a limited number of bursaries for individuals who demonstrate enterprise in overcoming their disability in a working environment over a period of time.

Funds have been raised to support the Trust through sponsorship and there have been some magnificent fund raising efforts by Northern Development Company. Recently a major appeal has been launched to raise £250,000 for a Revolving Loan Fund to assist disabled people to establish or expand their businesses. This initiative will row in very well with the expansion of the Northern Pinetree Trust and it is probably helpful that I am Chairman of both organisations.

I have not consciously been a firebrand in the movement that has raised awareness of disability across the country and I have never been in the forefront of any struggle, but perhaps by adding my voice or presence here and there I may have helped a little to make the general population recognise that disabled people are not much different from the rest and most of them only need a little help to enable them to lead full and satisfying lives. Over the thirty years or so since my accident I have seen huge strides made on this part of the human stage. No longer are we put in the guard's van, we are now helped into our seat. Far fewer are the occasions when we have to be bodily lifted up several steps into a building to gain access, although there are still many old buildings which are inaccessible to wheelchairs. More needs to be done and there are now some splendidly thriving organisations like the Spinal Injuries Association, of which Lady Masham is a founder member and President, which campaigns fearlessly for the things which still need to be done to give disabled people an equal chance. At the same time it provides practical help to its members, who all suffer from spinal cord damage and have immediate problems of daily living.

All the time different initiatives are trying to improve the lot of disabled people. For example I am even now participating in a comparative evaluation of catheters used for Intermittent Catheterisation, a new method of emptying the bladder which made a great deal of difference to my life when I started it in 1990. I believe this evolutionary process will go on, and as it moves forward the gap between disabled and able bodied people will narrow to the benefit of both.

17

A Senior Partner

Experience is the name everyone gives to his mistakes.
Oscar Wilde

 SUPPOSE THAT THERE COULD BE SOME considerable debate on the question of when one can be classed a 'senior
partner'. It is generally assumed that it occurs when one
reaches the age of fifty and one is serving on the Executive
Committee of the firm. I joined the Committee in 1975 when I was 43
and served for nine years, and therefore assume that it was at some point
in this period that I reached the exalted state. In fact, when I *was* fifty, I
was asked to serve as deputy to John Darby, the senior partner of the
firm, with responsibility for liaising with the offices outside London.

What is the role of a senior partner? In my view, he is either prominent
in the community in which he is based or he is a high level, much regarded
specialist in a niche area of the practice. In either case, he must be available
to give advice to his colleagues and be capable of mature argument and
debate.

I belonged to the first category and was particularly active in various
areas of life that affected the practice, most of which have already been
covered in previous chapters. My role in Business in the Community and
with the Enterprise Agencies, my role as Honorary Treasurer of the
University, as a Director of the Regional Health Authority and on the
board of Northern Electric gave me a visibility as a senior partner which
benefited the firm. My high profile with various disablity organisations
gave it added purpose, and my position as one of the founders of the
Tyne and Wear Foundation enhanced the caring image which I wanted
the firm to show. When I was asked to chair the Northern Finance Forum
in 1989 (a sort of Noah's Ark comprising two prominent members of
each of the numerate professions) a certain *gravitas* was also added.

In 1988 I returned from my second sabbatical, having been away for
over two months, to find a letter waiting from the Palace appointing me
OBE. A day or so later the Lord Lieutenant, Sir Ralph Carr-Ellison, called

to see me to invite me to become a Deputy Lieutenant of Tyne and Wear. The combination of both honours landing on me together was rather unusual and certainly helped my visibility in a way I had not foreseen! The office of Lord Lieutenant dates back to the reign of Henry VIII and gave him powers to defend his country, and shortly afterwards empowered him to appoint Deputy Lieutenants who were required to raise six hundred Pike Men. Even today the Lord Lieutenant is concerned with the Reserve Forces and Deputy Lieutenants act in accordance with his wishes. Occasionally I stand in for the Lord Lieutenant, generally on naval matters because I am one of only two naval Deputy Lieutenants in my county. My OBE was presented to me by Her Majesty the Queen in Buckingham Palace in the autumn. Sue, Mark and Nicola all accompanied me to attend the ceremony, following which I gave a rather jolly lunch party at the Connaught for several old friends.

By 1991 I had become one of the father figures within the profession and when, in May of that year, I was given the Founding Society's Award, I felt that there was really nothing more that I could do to add to my visibility. A week later, however, I was honoured by Newcastle University who conferred on me the Honorary Degree of Doctor of Civil Law at a moving ceremony faultlessly conducted in the Kings Hall of the University. I felt strangely academic dressed up in my robes and was conscious that I was holding up the procession on my crutches, but I felt inordinately proud and it made up, in some measure, for missing Cambridge.

The demands made by the role of a senior partner meant that one spent rather less time with one's clients, although junior partners and senior managers took on some of the load and provided a great deal of support. I enjoyed working with my clients as much as any aspect of professional life and I valued the close working relationship and mutual respect which came from years of working together and really understanding their problems. I would always try and find time to encourage managers to develop themselves and their careers. One of the great causes of satisfaction is to see people whom I have worked with at all levels of the firm now running the firm as partners in different offices throughout the country. As with most businesses the structure is like a pyramid and spillage becomes normal as the top of the pyramid contracts: this is felt most noticeably at manager level and I would try to give a helping hand wherever possible.

A senior partner is expected to do a fair amount of entertaining, some of it formal, in the office, some of it informal, outside. Many accountants use the golf course as a venue for entertaining. Because of my accident I was unable to do this, but because I was able to shoot I would often invite

Appointment as Deputy Lieutenant by Sir Ralph Carr-Ellison, Lord Lieutenant.

clients and friends who were influential in helping the firm to shoot with me. The Accountants' Dinner was regarded as something which the firm should use as a vehicle for entertaining. I decided that if we were going to do it, we should do it properly and thus instituted a pre-dinner champagne reception at the Northern Counties Club to get the evening off on a high note. I think this tradition is still maintained, although today I attend the dinner in my capacity as a past President along with other past Presidents.

In 1989 my firm Arthur Young merged with Ernst & Whinney to create Ernst & Young. This was the first merger of two of the previous "Big Eight" accounting firms and in part was due to a wish to pre-empt other mergers which might occur, leaving our firms isolated. We had talked to each other in the USA and the UK for a number of years and when our Executive Committee met the Americans at Sea Island in 1976 we had identified Ernst & Whinney as our natural defensive ally. On a world-wide level the merger created a huge firm, certainly one of the Big Three and in the UK it worked very well. Ernst & Whinney was tightly controlled from the centre, whilst Arthur Young had devolved more autonomy to the office managing partners. As a result, Ernst & Whinney was the more efficient, with the partners of Arthur Young generally showing greater initiative. The merger thus created an interesting blend of abilities. Ernst & Whinney also had a very powerful and prestigious audit practice whilst Arthur Young had the best tax practice in the UK. In Newcastle we had a happy merger. John Stanley, my opposite number, was an old friend and had followed me, two years on, as President of the Northern Society in 1981. We got on very well together and that, I am sure, set the tone for the new office – although it was some time before we were able to get everyone under one roof. Geoff Norman became Managing Partner, which left only one problem: we had two Insolvency partners and only needed one. Roger Griffiths stayed and went on to become President of the Northern Society. Alan Marlor, my protégé, went to Leeds to head up our Yorkshire Insolvency practice. Sadly he left the firm a few years later. Overall, however, the merger seems to have worked very well. Geoff Norman is now the Regional Managing Partner for the Midlands and Peter Willey, our tax partner, is now the Newcastle Managing Partner – although he still keeps an eye on my personal tax affairs, thank goodness!

Practice development is something with which a senior partner must involve himself and this might take the form of targeted entertaining or, more generally, assisting the firm to get across its message of expertise in specific areas. In recent years it has been the practice among companies who are thinking of changing their auditors to invite contending firms to present in competition with one another (a beauty parade!). Towards the end of my life in practice I took part in several such presentations where an ability to speak was certainly an asset.

I retired from the firm on 30 June 1992, to the accompaniment of many speeches and the popping of many corks.

18

Retirement

Superfluous lags the veteran on the stage.
Samuel Johnson

FTER THE CELEBRATIONS that marked my retirement at the end of June in 1992 and the family holiday in Cornwall, I returned to the office to find that nothing much had changed. I was very kindly allowed to keep my office and the use of my secretary, and for nearly three years I was given some form of secretarial assistance. In fact, even today, the managing partner's secretary will always help me with the church accounts or whatever else needs doing. I can't think highly enough of the way in which my former partners continue to succour me in my old age. But for the last two years I have worked mainly from my study at home with the aid of a fax machine.

I handed over all my clients when I retired but I still meet many of them in the 'village' that is Newcastle upon Tyne. As I have indicated many of them have become very good friends based upon the mutual respect of an excellent professional relationship.

Over the years since I retired from the office I have also resigned from or completed most of my public appointments, although I am still a director of one or two companies. I am still very interested in naval matters and attend dinners in *Calliope* when I can, but I have given up the position of secretary of the Retired Officers Association and I resigned from the TAVRA Committee when I retired from the firm.

However, I do have some new interests. I was greatly honoured when, in June 1995, I was sworn in as an Honorary Freeman of Newcastle upon Tyne Trinity House. The origins of Trinity House go back to 1505 and probably much earlier, but the "house" in Broad Chare has been occupied since then by the Guild or Fraternity of the Blessed Trinity of Newcastle upon Tyne, for the annual rent of a red rose! Trinity House received its first Royal Charter on 5 October 1536 from King Henry VIII, whereupon it was empowered to levy dues on ships arriving on the River Tyne. Further Royal Charters followed in the next hundred years or so, during which time the House greatly helped the improvement of navigation in and around the ports of the North East of England. It established buoys and beacons, licensed masters, mates and pilots, and advised on and oversaw improvements within the various rivers and ports. Over the years these powers and duties have been diminished but the historical signifi-cance of Trinity House remains and it still examines, licenses and administers North Sea deep sea pilots, together with the Trinity Houses of Hull and London. It also has an educational and training role with sea cadets and sea scouts, and is dedicated to the preservation of its heritage and traditions and the maintenance of the wonderful old buildings on the quayside of Newcastle, which it is fortunate enough to own. I was made an Honorary Freeman together with Nigel Sherlock and Sir David Chapman, all of us former High Sheriffs of Tyne and Wear, because we advised the brethren when they lost their main source of income from inshore buoyage, which ceased in 1993. On our advice and with our active assistance an appeal was launched to raise funds for Trinity House so that it could become much more widely used and its beautiful rooms exposed to public view. This has been achieved through a system of associate members, each of whom is entitled to bring parties of between fifty and one hundred people to the house.

In 1996 I became a trustee of the Newburn Sea Cadets and I also became a steward of the Hostman's Company – one of the ancient Guilds of Freemen of the City. This is particularly interesting as it gives me an

Trinity House: being made an Honorary Freeman of Newcastle upon Tyne.

insight into the interaction between the Freemen and the Corporation of Newcastle. I had been sworn in as a Freeman in 1983, having served articles with Percy Cooper as a Scrivener.

My overriding concern with disability issues has meant that I have retained my connections with Disability North, The Calvert Trust and the Pinetree Trust. A considerable part of my time is taken up with these organisations and I do find it difficult sometimes not having a secretary. I also continue to serve on the Community Affairs panel of Northern Electric PLC and on the board of Newcastle St Cuthbert Estates Ltd. In 1996 I handed over the chair of Northern Football Ground Company Ltd to John Ward although I retained a seat on the board. I am still the auditor of St Nicholas Church in Gosforth, the ancient parish church which dates back to AD 1200 and earlier.

Retirement is supposed to bring more time to indulge in one's hobbies. I don't seem to have much more time but I am still able to do a little painting and fishing in the summer, and shooting in the winter. As I get older, I cannot be quite as active as I used to be but I can still row a boat. Regular massage and occasional visits to the chiropractor also keep me in good shape. I have changed from a 12 bore to a 20 bore shot gun to lessen the strain on my shoulders and this certainly seems to have helped a great deal. As far as fishing is concerned, I find that I cannot use a big 15' salmon rod for more than three quarters of an hour at a stretch, so trout fishing is now my favourite summer occupation.

Holidays in France seem even in better in retirement because there are no time pressures – or very few – and one can wander more freely. In 1993 Sue and I had a memorable holiday in Zimbabwe. Zimbabwe is a beautiful country and we found the Zimbabweans a friendly and easy-going people. Victoria Falls was even better in real life than in all of the pictures we had seen and we very much enjoyed visiting the Queen Elizabeth VI Special School in Bulawayo and talking to some of the children there who were about to visit the Calvert Trust. We saw them later, at Keswick, and they were indeed a truly wonderful bunch, although most were very disabled.

I had served my year as President of Northern back in 1978/79 but for most of the time since then had acted as Chairman of Northern Football Ground Co Ltd, which owned McCracken Park. I was in the chair when we made a momentous decision in the middle of the 1990s to sell a pitch and rebuild the clubhouse, and have now handed over the chair to John Ward, whose father, like mine, was responsible for Northern when McCracken Park was built before the war.

One of the blessings of retirement is that there is more time to play bridge, which both Sue and I enjoy very much. I play in two men's fours and Sue has at least three ladies' fours. We also enjoy playing occasional mixed bridge. One of our favourite forms of entertaining is to have a couple for supper and bridge.

Generally, I enjoy being retired. There is a bit more time for everything – particularly getting up in the morning which I find as an older paraplegic takes me much longer than it used to do. If I need an early start I need to be well prepared the night before. There is more time to plan the day, the week and the months ahead – and I do enjoy planning! I find it very easy to fill every day and consciously have to choose priorities. And since Sue and I got married for better or worse but not for lunch, I also try and ensure a lunchtime visit to my club once or twice a week.

In the autumn of 1993 we started preparing for the following year: in 1994 I was to have a temporary break from the pressure-free pleasures of retirement in order to take on the mantle of High Sheriff. A very busy year was in prospect.

19

High Sheriff

 HE OFFICE OF HIGH SHERIFF is one of the most ancient secular offices in the country. It has long been associated with the forces of law and order and, more recently, with the public services generally. Tyne and Wear, of course, is a relatively new county and its High Sheriff has only been in existence since 1974, although prior to this the city of Newcastle had boasted its own Sheriff for 374 years. Tyne and Wear, however, was formed from pieces shorn off Northumberland and Durham. The first High Sheriff of Northumberland was appointed in 1076 and that of Durham in 1100.

The word 'sheriff' is derived from Shire Reeve. Shire means something shorn off from a large unit, in this case a county from a country. And a Reeve was the man in charge. There is some uncertainty as to when the first sheriff was appointed. References to "High Reeve" and "Shire Man" can be found earlier but the Shrievalty Association (the trade union of High Sheriffs) decided that 992 was the date. There was a great deal of celebration up and down the country in 1992, to mark the millennium of the office.

From the tenth century a High Sheriff has been appointed to each shire, or county, in England and Wales, originally to be responsible for its entire administration – financial, military and judicial. He was policeman, judge (sharing judicial duites with the Bishop), general, recruiter, fireman and tax collector all in one. Indeed, in the early history of the shrievalty, the sheriffs of the northern counties occupied a particularly privileged position because the responsibility to defend the border necessitated that they should be allowed considerable freedom of action in military and financial matters.

Over the centuries, various monarchs and parliaments have reduced the powers of the High Sheriff which were further diluted with the creation

of the office of Lord Lieutenant in 1557, but the office is still going strong
and I hope that the position will continue for another thousand years.
Although stripped of most of his ancient powers, the High Sheriff retains
today some important responsibilities, including the execution of High
Court writs, and acting as presiding officer at parliamentary elections
within his bailiwick. He is particularly concerned with the well-being of
Her Majesty's High Court judges when they come to Newcastle on circuit.
Above all, he stands as the Queen's representative in his county for the
promotion of the rule of law and the support of all agencies and activities
connected with law enforcement and crime prevention.

I was approached by Nigel Sherlock in the spring of 1990 with the
suggestion that I should allow my name to be considered for nomination
of High Sheriff of Tyne and Wear. After discussing it with Sue, I readily
agreed to the proposition. We made it our business to be in London in
November 1991 to attend the reading of the Roll in the Court of the Lord
Chief Justice, which was the first time that my appointment had been
made public.

In the summer of 1992 Sue and I gave some thought as to how I might
manage in Court dress, in view of my disability. The dress itself was no
problem since I was able to borrow that from Ted Wrangham, who had
been High Sheriff of Northumberland some years previously, but I certainly could not wear the traditional slipper. The problem was solved by
Lobbs of St James who have made my boots for me for the last twenty
years. They devised a pair of patent leather boots together with black
suede gaiters incorporating the traditional buckle. It took eighteen months
for them to make the boots to their and my satisfaction and they cost as
much as a new dress uniform! With about six months to go I started
planning in earnest and organised the printing, getting excellent service
from Reed Print and Design. I familiarised myself with the role of High
Sheriff by reading the appropriate texts, in particular Irene Gladwin's
"The Sheriff: The Man and His Office", and the beautifully bound Diary
kept by the Tyne and Wear High Sheriffs. Sue and I were given extremely
efficient briefings by Sir David Chapman, my predecessor and his wife
Marika. In the run up to our installation, Barbara Lyndon-Skeggs, the
High Sheriff elect of Northumberland and I were entertained to lunch by
our respective Under Sheriffs and were again briefed and discussed together the year ahead. Barbara and I got on very well and we had a very
happy year together. There were various meetings concerned with the
installation ceremony itself and I had by now become heavily involved
with my predecessor raising money to set up a permanent High Sheriff's
Awards Fund.

In court dress as High Sheriff, with Sue and Rusty at Graham Park Road.

I embarked on my year of High Sheriff with several objectives, aiming to add specific purpose to my time in office. My first objective was to improve the relationship with the city of Newcastle. We got on extremely well with the Lady Mayoress Joan Lamb and also with Bob Brown (and his wife Marjorie) when he became Lord Mayor in 1994. A good working relationship waas established with Geoff Cook the Chief Executive, and with other officers. The presentation of a Shrievalty Millennium plate to the city at the Dagger Dinner in February 1995 completed the process and I believe that the relationship is very soundly based. Secondly, I wished to complete the fund raising for the Awards Fund which David Chapman and I had started in November 1993, aiming for a target of £200,000. It is now clear that the High Sheriff Awards are here to stay and have become a useful adjunct to the High Sheriff's role of supporting the rule of law.

My third objective was to assist in the battle against crime in any way possible. I readily accepted the invitation of Tony Hill, the Chairman of the Northumbria Coalition Against Crime, to join his Board in the summer of 1994. When Sir David Chapman accepted the Chairmanship of the Coalition I told him that I would stay on the board after my term of office had finished. Fourthly, I was determined to help with networking and to show the flag of the High Sheriff in as many parts of Tyne and Wear as possible. I maintained the tradition of holding receptions in each of the five Boroughs of the County. I held a joint reception in Trinity House with the High Sheriff of Northumberland, two buffet lunch parties at home and a reception for the ethnic community in the Dene Centre. I generally spoke at these receptions in order to get the Shrieval message over, but kept it brief and tried to be amusing. My final objective was to try and achieve maximum publicity for the office of High Sheriff. In this respect I was only moderately successful, although Ernst & Young allowed me the use of their PR consultant. I suspect that this may have been because the High Sheriff is largely associated with good news; the press, unfortunately, tends to favour bad.

I had decided to have my Installation in the Civic Centre of Newcastle upon Tyne partly because no other High Sheriff had been sworn in there before and partly because I wanted to cement the rapport between the Tyne and Wear Shrievalty and the City (when Tyne and Wear was formed in 1974 Newcastle lost its Sheriff and for several years there were strained relationships). When it was suggested to Joan Lamb that I should be sworn in in her Civic Centre she readily agreed and sat at the top table at the Installation Ceremony, which was conducted by Sir Mark Waller, an old friend and a High Court Judge. Trumpets which had belonged to Sir David Chapman's grandfather were blown expertly by two trumpeters from the Royal Northumberland Fusiliers. Approximately 250 guests witnessed the Installation and attended a reception in the Banqueting Hall afterwards. Later that same evening Sue and I hosted a supper party at home.

There were several other formal occasions during the year, particularly the formal opening of the Law Courts at the start of the legal year on October 4, where the High Sheriff of Northumberland and I, together with our Under Sheriffs and Chaplains, met two High Court judges on the steps of the Law Court with a fanfare of trumpets blown by four trumpeters from the Police Band. Unfortunately the extremely low ceiling and subdued lights of the Law Courts inside the building was something of a let down after the impressive ceremony outside. On Armistice Day I marched with the Mayorial party to a service at the Cenotaph in Eldon

Square and later joined the Lord Mayor for refreshments at the Royal British Legion.

Mainly because of my disability I decided to engage a part-time chauffeur for my year and with the aid of the Chief Constable identified a recently retired police sergeant, Fred Patterson, who proved absolutely invaluable not only as a chauffeur but also as an extra pair of hands, helping, for example, to move my stool around for me at functions and receptions.

Sue had announced from the outset that she wanted to deal with all our entertaining requirements and her partner Virginia Steer was a tremendous help in assisting her with the task. Indeed, I suspect that we managed to feed the whole of Tyne and Wear during my year in office! I was also indebted to Richard Granger for providing an excellent drinks service at all of my receptions. Ernst & Young were most generous in allowing me to retain my room and the use of a secretary, Adele Jameson, who assisted unstintingly with the administrative load throughout the year. Like my predecessor I asked Bill Meikle to be my Under Sheriff and his advice and support were greatly appreciated. The preparation of invitation lists for different receptions, gathering information and deciding who should be on them was one of the biggest tasks and I had not appreciated, beforehand, how time-consuming it would be. Entertaining judges is one of the High Sheriff's main tasks. We entertained twenty five judges to dinner during the year, each of whom had to be written to and the appropriate guests gathered together. This is a substantial task which took up a considerable amount of time. Part of the objective was to give the judges an insight into life in the North East because, on the whole, they were not familiar with this part of the country. On every occasion the conversation flowed back and forth and I am sure that the judges and our guests enjoyed those dinner parties.

In the summer of 1994 I visited the Low Newton Remand Centre for Young Offenders and the Frankland High Security Prison nearby, both in Co. Durham but with a large number of inmates from Tyne and Wear. I invited Mr Justice Owen and Mr Justice Potts to join me at Frankland because I felt that they might meet some old friends – which, indeed, they did. I was particularly interested in the psychiatric services which my City Health Trust was providing to the inmates, and spent a useful hour with the medical staff there. Afterwards we all had a discussion with the governor which was most enlightening, and the judges then invited me to join them for supper at the Judges' Lodgings at nearby Plawsworth afterwards.

One of the principal duties of the High Sheriff is to greet the judges when they first attend court. My first judge was Sir William Macpherson of Cluny and Blairgowrie, who had to judge the notorious "Black" case – a very difficult case which was based entirely on circumstantial evidence, although I do not think that anyone who attended had any doubt about the guilt of Mr Black. Thirteen weeks had been set aside for the case but in the event it only lasted six weeks. I attended on three occasions and was struck by the extraordinary command, coupled with courtesy, with which the judge controlled proceedings. I sat with most of the judges although in some of the matrimonial cases the presence of a High Sheriff was not always welcomed by the protagonists.

During the year there were a number of Church Parades which it was customary for the High Sherrif to attend. On June 5th, there was an exceptional Parade in commemoration of D-Day with substantial numbers of the Regular and Reserve Forces marching through the city and a flypast by the RAF, following a service in the cathedral. Sue and I attended with the Lord Lieutenant, the Duchess of Northumberland and the Lord Mayor and there was an enjoyable lunch in the Mansion House afterwards. We attended a Trinity Sunday Service in Trinity House which is the traditional service going back a very long time indeed. It was followed by a buffet lunch in the beautiful banqueting room at Trinity House and was a great occasion. The Legal Service in Durham Cathedral in July was very memorable, followed by a reception on the lawn of Durham Castle – made all the more pleasant by brilliant sunshine and an accompanying band – and an excellent lunch in the Great Hall hosted by the High Sheriff of Durham. The Legal Service in York Minster was as well done as ever under the leadership of Richard Howard-Vyse, the High Sheriff of West Yorkshire and was followed by an excellent lunch in the Assembly Rooms. It was too far for me to march with the other High Sheriffs to the Assembly Rooms and back again but I did manage to join in the march at the West Door of the Minster.

I was very lucky in having several Royal Naval ships in the Tyne during my year. *HMS Northumberland* finished building in Swan Hunters early in my term of office. We attended her farewell party and then helped to entertain her officers when she returned in December. *HMS Newcastle* visited during the summer and when the ship's company marched through the city to the Civic Centre (having been given the freedom of the city) the Lord Mayor very kindly asked me to share the dais with him for the salute. We also had a very popular visit from *HMS Ark Royal*, which included a memorable private lunch party with the captain. Another splendid evening was spent on board a Dutch Naval Squadron. Sue and I also developed a strong rapport with Group Captain Tim Willbond, the Commanding Officer of RAF Boulmer which we visited several times.

We had several royal visits during the year, including three from the Princess Royal who was indefatigable in her capacity to manage several engagements during the day. On one occasion in December there were three royal visits in five days, but perhaps the most notable was that of His Majesty King Harold of Norway, when he came in March 1995 to receive an Honorary Degree from Newcastle University. This was a particularly nostalgic occasion because he received the same degree that I had done shortly before: Doctor of Civil Law. I could have marched in the procession wearing my academic robes but of course I was in Court dress.

During my year I had to make several awards. My colleague Barbara Lyndon-Skeggs and I had two sessions presenting Court Awards to members of the public who had been awarded specific sums by judges for bravery or other selfless acts in the public interest. I also presented medals to the Newburn Sea Cadets and on four separate evenings Long Service Medals to members of the Tyne and Wear Fire Service. I opened the Disabled North Exhibition in Gateshead and, later in the year, presented the Sir David Chapman Cup for the Most Outstanding Police Officer of the year.

Throughout the year I regularly attended numerous receptions and dinners and I became a familiar face at the Mansion House where I was always received most graciously.

Perhaps one of the most amusing and different occasions was the installation of Rabbi Francis Berry at the United Reformed Synagogue in Gosforth. I had always thought that it was not *de rigueur* for Jews to drive to the synagogue but the United Reformed branch obviously thought differently because a large car park was situated just beside the building. I had remembered that it was not correct to enter the synagogue bare headed and I had brought along my splendid High Sheriff's 'fore and aft' hat which I was able to wear for the first (and only) time. Unfortunately the Lord Mayor, who also attended the ceremony with me, had forgotten to bring his and was obliged to don a borrowed skull cap.

I visited as many people as time allowed throughout the year, making formal calls on the Chief Executive of Newcastle and the Chief Executive of Sunderland – the two cities in my parish. I was particularly concerned to know more about the work that the Probation Service and the police were doing, and undertook various journeys and expeditions with both of those forces. I got quite close to the Fire Service, who do a wonderful job in Tyne and Wear and who are often under attack from a small minority of hooligans.

Tyne and Wear is not like a shire county where the High Sheriff

Receiving my Honorary Degree.

traditionally gives a large garden party. I held receptions in each of the five boroughs of Tyne and Wear: the two cities of Newcastle and Sunderland, also Gateshead, North Tyneside and South Tyneside. All were extremely well attended and each was different in character. On each occasion I attended in Court Dress so that the High Sheriff could be seen, as he has been for so many years. I spoke to my guests about the work of the High Sheriff and any other relevant matters. Particularly moving was my reception in North Tyneside, late in my year, when among the guests were two of the award winners of the High Sheriff's Award, and I was able to introduce them to the assembled company. This encouraged lively conversation for the rest of the reception.

I was extremely surprised to learn that there were over 50,000 citizens of ethnic origin within my parish. Consequently I gave a reception specifically for them. I had invited the Lord Lieutenant to join me so that we could both give an account of ourselves and what we did, but unfortunately he was unable to attend at the last minute, so I had to speak for both of us. I believe that this reception was well received and did something to break down the barriers which still exist in our society today.

One of those attending was Peter Chen, the doyen of the Chinese community, who wrote a charming thank you letter inviting us to dine with him at the Dragon House in Chinatown. We had a wonderful evening and he has become a true friend. We were delighted when he was appointed MBE last year.

In former times the City of Newcastle used to give what became known as "dagger money" to the judges coming to Newcastle so that they could buy protection for themselves when travelling to and from the Newcastle assizes to another part of the country, particularly Carlisle. Today, this old custom is remembered with a "Dagger Dinner", and Sue and I will always regard it as a great privilege to have attended this historic occasion. We were entertained with a wonderful speech by Sir John Laws who received the traditional "dagger money".

Perhaps the most moving ceremony of all was the High Sheriff's Awards Ceremony. This took place in February 1995 in the Kings Hall of Newcastle University. There was a very high standard of entries and it was lucky that we were able to find a clear outright winner who received the first award of £5,000. We were also able to give ten subsidiary awards of £500. Because the event was sponsored in this year by British Telecom we were able to roll up the interest on the Awards Fund and take it closer to the target of £200,000, most of which had been raised by Sir David Chapman and myself from our personal contacts in local industry and among local trusts. The ceremony was impressive and was raised to considerable heights by an address by Robert Swan, the famous explorer, who happened to be a patron of the winner, Peak Leisure of Sunderland.

In earlier months I had made many visits throughout the county to check out the applications in some detail and we had had a long meeting of the panel to discuss the applications before arriving at our decisions about the winners. Although the amounts we gave out were not particularly substantial, they did make a difference in raising the profile among the voluntary sector in the battle against crime, and particularly youth crime.

Near the end of the year our old friend Janet Smith, new Presiding Judge of the North East Circuit, was sitting in Newcastle and came to stay for a weekend with her husband Robin. We invited John Stevens the Chief Constable and his wife Cynthia to join us, and enjoyed a good, old fashioned Sunday lunch free from cares and worries, although it did provide an opportunity for Janet and John Stevens to get to know one another; a good example, I think, of the High Sheriff at work 'behind the scenes'.

Our whole year passed very quickly and Sue and I enjoyed it a great deal. It is a truism that you can only get out of something what you put into it but the hard work of undertaking the job of High Sheriff is, I believe, more than repaid by meeting so many interesting people and having the satisfaction of having done a good job and helped to maintain the traditions of the office.

20

Business As Usual

Growing old is no more than a bad habit
which a busy man has no time to form.
André Maurois

N FEBRUARY 1997 WE SET OFF on a well-planned and long awaited holiday to South Africa, which Bruce Ruffman, our travel agent, had specially arranged with John Knighton of Southern Africa Travel. Nostalgically we started out at the Victoria Falls Hotel which had had a facelift since we had last stayed there five years previously. Our pleasure on this occasion was somewhat diminished by the loss of our luggage on the part of South Africa Airlines. However, it caught up with us the next day and we did enjoy the much improved Zimbabwe wines and excellent food on offer. We borrowed a chair from the hotel and a taxi took us to the car park near the Falls. The taxi driver pushed me down the track leading to the Falls which were magnificently in full flow. However, I think the rough journey was the last straw for the chair which shed a wheel later that day – luckily just outside our bedroom. A replacement was found, but suffered the same fate. The hotel's last remaining wheelchair held together just long enough to get me to the Blue Train at the back of the hotel the next morning, before it collapsed on the platform. Someone must have had quite a job repairing the hotel's wheelchairs for the next disabled guest.

The philosophy of the staff aboard the Blue Train was to pamper their guests; champagne flowed from the moment we boarded at 11.00am and never stopped. The food was exciting, original and served with excellent South African wines. A few hours south from Victoria Falls we stopped to get into open vehicles for a game drive at Hwangi. Soon after setting off it started to rain, so we had to put on oilskins which were provided. Because of the recent rains there was not much big game around, but we saw literally hundreds of different species of wild birds. We returned to the train wet through, but were able to take a bath in our private bathroom. Then, as the train sped on towards Bulawayo, we were able to

enjoy a wonderful dinner looking out at the darkening evening sky gradually snuffing out the rich forest colours which flashed past. We stopped
in Bulawayo for part of the night in order to get some peaceful rest before
speeding further south. When we awoke the next morning to a glorious
sunny day it was to find that we were approaching the Botswana border
(this was a change of plan and an unexpected bonus). As we travelled
further we were able to catch sight of plenty of game in the savannah to
the west. The view changed constantly and there was evidence of gold
and coal mining. And then, after breakfast, we went through Francistown
– the first sign of civilisation in Botswana. We noticed that, as in Zimbabwe, the children were all very well dressed. Throughout the day we
met several of our fellow travellers in the bar and from them learned
something of conditions in South Africa. One group of Swiss men seemed
to spend the entire day in the bar, drinking the South African equivalent
of advocaat but never appearing to suffer the effects! After dinner that
evening we turned east, towards Johannesburg. The quality of the rail-
tracks appeared to deteriorate now, and on that second night we did not
sleep as well. The following morning we stopped at a halt to the west of
Johannesburg and were bundled into taxis which sped us to the airport
(to the east of the city). We just made the flight to Nelspruit in the Eastern
Transvaal. There a hire car awaited us and we drove to Cybele Forest
Lodge, a peaceful retreat in the hills surrounded by plantations of coffee
and timber. At its centre was a charming old farmhouse with a wide
verandah, where we ate. But we slept in our own house, with our own
lovely garden and swimming pool. A decanter of sherry was provided
each evening in our elegant sitting room with a plate of cocktail savouries.
It was a very special place, and we enjoyed our days there. We also met
a charming couple, Peter and Gill Smith, who farmed on the Isle of Thanet
in Kent, and with whom we dined most nights. One day we took a
helicopter trip up the Blyde River Canyon and had a picnic in our
shirtsleeves on top of World's View, at 5,000 feet. The scenery in this part
of South Africa is really stunning.

It was a very easy drive down from the hills of the Eastern Transvaal
to the Mala Mala Game Reserve on the edge of the Kruger. We stayed at
Kirkmans Kamp (named after Harry Kirkman, one of South Africa's
foremost conservationists) which had in former times been a hunting
lodge, then a cattle ranch and is now an exclusive safari park of 45,000
acres, housing only twenty guests. We met some interesting people and
had several memorable game drives in specially adapted vehicles, with a
ranger and a tracker, and saw virtually all kinds of African big game. It
was extremely exciting rounding a corner of the track and coming face

to face with a fully grown elephant. Even more exciting was going off-track into the bush, and charging after a pride of lions, with branches and thorns whipping the side of the vehicle. Particularly memorable were a night drive with spotlights, just behind four hunting male lions, and our ranger's expertise in driving the vehicle on the top of some huge rocks overlooking the Sand River, with a female leopard – quite stationary – sitting within fifteen yards of us, as sunset faded. A little later we were having our sundowners close to our vehicle, discussing the evening's excitement.

We then paid a short visit to the Drackensburg Mountains and visited the Giant's Castle country park. Here we had our only bad experience in South Africa. Having driven miles out across open countryside we went through a township just as the local school was closing for the day. We were ambushed by about thirty children concealed in a hollow in the road. They opened the back door, where Sue's handbag was lying in view. Fortunately, Sue was able to accelerate as I beat of the attackers with one of my crutches. An unpleasant and salutary experience.

We flew from Durban to Capetown and spent a luxurious week at the Mount Nelson Hotel, relaxing and enjoying what must be the most disabled-friendly swimming pool anywhere in the world, with two hand-rails leading down gentle steps into the pool, set in delightful gardens with a backdrop of Table Mountain peeping over the top of the hotel building. We hired another car and drove round the Cape, meeting (as Geordies are wont to do) old friends Graeme and Nancy Anderson on the very tip of the Cape of Good Hope. They had booked a table for lunch at the Lighthouse Restaurant, and kindly invited us to join them. Back at the Mount Nelson Hotel we bumped into several other people we knew, and realised that we were not that far from home!

The last part of our African journey took us to the winelands, where we stayed at a small hotel outside Paarl. We visited a family who lived on a charming small farm nearby, who were great friends of Sue's cousin William Dotchin, and from them learned something of the area. We visited and wine-tasted at excellent watering holes at Paarl, Stellenbosch and Franschoek. We had a glorious picnic at the Boschendal Estate near Franschoek which we had booked several days ahead, where we joined our fellow picnickers at tables decked with linen cloths under massive old oak trees on a lovely estate, and enjoyed the most fabulous food and wine on a warm summer's day. Perfection!

South Africa had proved to be a wonderful country and it was with great reluctance that we eventually drove to the airport for the journey home. However, nothing in this world is ever perfect: we nearly missed leaving South Africa all together, as I was abandoned in the first class lounge with no wheelchair! Organisational problems apart, I sincerely hope that South Africa will continue to move forward with the momentum established under Nelson Mandela's leadership, and that the deep wounds between black and white will ultimately be healed. From our perspective, and from what we saw in the places we frequented, we did not feel that integration in South Africa had been achieved, particularly in the hotels, in the same way as it had been in Zimbabwe.

During the three weeks that we had been in the country, both Sue and I had complained, from time to time, of feeling below par. We put it down to an excess of hospitality – for example, on the Blue Train – or to the dreaded malaria pills that we were obliged to take. Shortly after my return home, I visited my doctor. He was unable to pinpoint anything but made an appointment for me to see the consultant physician at the Freeman Hospital, who examined me three weeks later. He suspected a swelling in my spleen, which was confirmed by ultrasound. I had, in the meantime, been carrying out a series of Calvert Trust meetings over three successive weekends, broken only by Easter with Jane and Roger in Sussex. I can remember chairing a meeting of the Council of the Calvert Trust in Keswick which lasted some two and half hours, by the end of which I was feeling very ill. Further tests in hospital during the week commencing 21 April (my 65th birthday) revealed the severity of the problem with my spleen. Strangely enough, no other organs appeared to be showing signs of any abnormality. I had suspected that my liver might reveal evidence of some wear and tear, at least! The senior surgeon at the Freeman returned from the USA at the end of that week, and decided to remove the spleen. He gave me instructions to go home and enjoy myself for the weekend, and told me that he would operate on Monday morning. I was not feeling too bad over the weekend and we were able to go to Tom and Sally Fenwick's Ruby Wedding party, held in a grand marquee in their garden on the Sunday lunchtime, enjoying the time spent with them and many other old friends. Sue then dropped me at the Freeman on the Sunday evening. The operation lasted a long time and the spleen weighed seven and a half pounds. My surgeon came in to see me often in the first twenty four hours following the operation. Then there was a gap, until day four. He looked a bit glum, and I asked him what was the matter.

"The bad news first – it is cancer. The good news is that we can take care of this sort of cancer and you are just as likely to die of drink!"

He mapped out a programme of chemotherapy which would take most of the summer, saying that although he thought he had got rid of all the cancer when he removed the spleen, you could never be sure, and

chemotherapy would be belt and braces. He introduced me to his hae-
matologist, who then took over my treatment. I spent nine days in the
Freeman after the operation, during which time I realised that they had
little experience of dealing with paraplegics. The nurses seemed untrained
and it was left to the physios to get me on and off the loo. Before I left,
I was taken to a staircase and given an exam in walking up and down
stairs to make sure that I would be able to cope when I got home.

It was a long summer – or seemed so. It was not very hot to start with
and in June we had the worst rain for many years, which decimated the
wild partridges and pheasants. I had my first chemotherapy on 12 May
and thereafter five large phials of poison were injected into my system
through veins in one of my arms at three weekly intervals – the minimum
interval necessary for the blood to recover and be ready for another
cleansing. The doctors were pleased that my system stood up so well to
this harsh regime. There were several side effects; nausea, mitigated by
some quite effective anti-sickness pills; losing my hair, which did not
worry me at all (although it has now grown back quite well, apart from
the places where it had been receding previously!); feeling generally unwell
and tired for the first two or three days, when Sue would spoil me by
bringing me breakfast in bed; nosebleeds which would occur round about
the seventh day – one of which occurred before a Lions v South Africa
match on television, which I watched with a bucket between my knees,
bleeding throughout the entire game!; diarrhoea (worse for a paraplegic
since there was no warning); bladder problems, again exacerbated by
being a paraplegic and having no control. The only side effect which has
lasted for a period of one month from the date of my last chemotherapy
is a rash of spots which do not itch but which have now been identified
as urticaria. I am still being treated for this condition but it does not
seem to be serious. For three weeks or so after the operation my taste
was most peculiar and I found I could only drink sweet wine. Drinking
Sauterne with beef felt rather odd! The operation itself took a lot out of
me and it took about three months before I could take serious exercise,
like fishing.

However, the rest of my life went on as before and while I was in
hospital I was organising a reception for SSAFA to launch a fund-raising
campaign. In the middle of June a meeting of several Calvert Trustees
took place in my home with Heather Mills, a former model who had lost
a leg, and we appointed her our London fund raiser. I put a bottle of
champagne on ice, packed it in a newspaper in my carrying briefcase and
visited Ralph Carr-Ellison, my Lord Lieutenant, in the Nuffield. I found
him in some disarray since his new hip had dropped out of place the day

before, but some cold champagne cheered him up. I was driving my car within a fortnight of coming out of hospital.

In April I had had to shelve all my plans for the summer, and most appointments had been cancelled. They were gradually rearranged and my life began to resume its normal hue. I do not think that I consciously faced up to having to fight cancer – it was just a matter of carrying on living, doing what was possible and not attempting to do what wasn't. Fishing in Scotland had to go by the board, but I managed some late fishing in Northumberland with Sue at Unthank, Craglough, Capheaton and Hallington. We got to the Races as guests of Northern Rock on the Friday of Race Week but I did not feel well enough to go to the Plate on the Saturday and thus missed the usual fine hospitality of Scottish and Newcastle Breweries and the cheerful company of Alastair Wilson. In early July I was well enough for Sue to leave me for a week. She went down to Cornwall with her sister Jane and I survived easily on my own, being invited out frequently. My first away trip was the August Bank Holiday, which we spent with Rosemary Lewin-Smith in her fine holiday home in North Norfolk, closely followed by my final chemotherapy. Sue and I then drove to France in September.

When we returned to England the grouse season was well underway – the best for some years. Despite being only one month old these hardy birds had survived the bad weather in June; they are, as a breed, well used to coping with inclement conditions providing they can get a reasonable start. I had bought a new Range Rover, but, more importantly, I was now able to shoot grouse from an elephant seat on the back of an ATV – a four wheel motorbike driven by a keeper, who would drive me beside my butt, camouflage the bike and then load for me. This added a new dimension to my shooting which gives me a great challenge. I decided, on advice from Mark and others, to try a 20 bore and Andrew Cowie took me down to see Ian Sowerby, whose father had taught me a great deal about shooting twenty years before. Ian was extremely patient with me; I persevered with the 20 bore and had a great shooting season.

In late October several of us went on a Calvert Trust reconnaissance to Lourdes in the Pyrenees. We were greatly helped by the presence of Matthew Festing and Peter Lloyd, both Calvert Trustees and both Grand Knights of Malta and regular visitors to Lourdes. Jean Buscail, also a Grand Knight, was a prominent member of the local community and we stayed in one of his hotels. He kindly gave up several days to show us the surrounding area, particularly the activity sites where sailing, canoeing, horse riding and winter sports were undertaken. It is the most lovely country and we have decided to run some pilot courses during 1998 to explore the practicality of using the facilities that exist in the area. The idea of a French Calvert Trust is most exciting but, if it is to come to pass, I believe that it will require the French to take ownership of it. Several centuries ago England owned a lot of that country, but these days I fear that the French would not take too well to a British-led Calvert Trust being implanted in their midst.

In late November I reported to the Freeman Hospital for a body scan and in due course I learnt that there was no trace of cancer. My haematologists have told me that I can now regard the episode as being over. There is every hope and expectation that it will not recur. Being somewhat cautious, I am not totally convinced but will take life as it comes. My situation appears to be much better, but things can change very quickly.

I was lucky to be able to carry on shooting through the winter, wet though it undoubtedly was. My Range Rover bore up wonderfully and only got stuck on the last day of the season, when I was stranded some way behind the line of guns. I took up the position of back gun and was fortunate to have a chance of a left and right, and even luckier to hit them both!

I became more and more involved with my other interests again, spending a considerable amount of time advising a company of which I am director on a take-over of a business of a similar size. It now seems that this is coming to fruition.

February brought altogether better weather to the North East of England, even though it was unseasonably mild. I went twice to Northern to see two excellent games of rugby and evidence of a growing confidence and team spirit both on and off the field. February is a time for lunch parties at weekends and my stocks of vintage burgundy started dwindling. The Pinetree Trust received a big boost when Tyneside TEC gave it £30,000 pump priming money and we got down to planning the future in detail, with our major appeal starting in the early summer. The Spirit of Enterprise Awards were more popular than ever with a strong entry and we celebrated with the winner at a memorable dinner at the Calvert Trust at the end of February.

The government had badly misjudged the mood in the country regarding country sports with a private member's bill proposing a ban on hunting going through the House of Commons. A Countryside March was held in London on the first Sunday in March. Sue and I went to London for this, both feeling strongly about the suggested infringement of our ability to take part in whatever countryside pursuits we wanted to enjoy. Sue marched with Roger Venables, her brother-in-law, while I sat outside my Club in Pall Mall dispersing refreshments to many chums whom I saw passing, and was joined by my old colleague Peter Smith, now living in Brighton, who had come up to see me, but also much enjoyed the occasion. We all had rather a late lunch in the Club, thus inevitably missing some friends who were passing by at the time. What struck me most was the good humour of the whole day. There was a huge turn out – estimated at something like 280,000 – and everyone processed along the route in a calm and dignified manner.

From London we went down to the South West and stayed with Ken and Gilli Frewer, old naval chums, having called on Hugh and Joyce Roland-Price for lunch on the way and gossiped about old times, not having seen them for a very long time. We also called to have lunch with John and Ursula Dornton and found John in good heart. We stayed in Devon at the Horn of Plenty for three days. The weather was extremely bad and we were denied the outstanding view from our bedroom window but there was exceptional food and wine and we spent a very happy evening entertaining Terry and Mary Thompson – more old naval chums. From there, we went down to Cornwall and stayed at the Nare Hotel, a marvellous old place stuck seemingly in a time warp. It was very luxurious and we had a great view of the rolling sea from our bedroom, with Nare Head standing stark and solid out in front. We had wonderful food, with cream teas and fine wines and even bridge organised for those who wanted it. It was a lovely quiet week, during which we explored the beautiful Roseland Peninsular, with the lovely church in the creek at St Just, the gardens at Trelissick and many other delights, with rhododendrons in full flower on account of the mild winter. We thought it was probably the best hotel we had ever stayed in and I think that March is a lovely time to visit that part of the world, normally so crowded.

From Cornwall we came up to Exmoor and stayed with Edwin and Michaela Beckett for the Calvert Exmoor Trustees meeting. The Becketts have a lovely home on the eastern edge of the moor and on the Saturday night they gave a dinner party for us, which included Jim Thompson, the Lord Bishop of Bath and Wells who, I discovered, was a chartered accountant and by an amazing coincidence had also won the Founding Society's Award some three years after me. The following weekend was the Calvert Trust Conference at Kielder which was extremely well attended and where there was great enthusiasm. It was very hectic for me in particular because I had to fit in several side meetings and chair a meeting of the Council of the Calvert Trust during the weekend – made memorable by an excellent party given by the Charlton family in their lovely home at Hesleyside Hall, some eighteen years after they had hosted the party for us there introducing the Calvert Trust to the locals in the North Tyne valley. Most of the weekend was spent looking at ourselves from outside, with speakers to prompt us. Although there are many problems to overcome, I believe the Calvert Trust now has a solid base and can face the future with confidence.

Mark and I held our usual clay pigeon shoot on the old communist Bank Holiday Monday, May 4th. Fortune and the sun shone on us and we made £2,000 for the Julie Kent Trust in aid of Cystic Fibrosis in the North East. A week or so earlier we had had a preliminary planning meeting with Ann Galbraith – until recently chair of the RVI – and several of the staff primarily involved with cystic fibrosis about the possibility of launching a major appeal to raise funds for a dedicated cystic fibrosis unit in the RVI. The ball has been left in their court to decide on precisely what is wanted in the way of accommodation but I am determined to make this appeal succeed and will take steps to set it up properly when the time comes. Having a granddaughter with cystic fibrosis I have more than a passing interest in the subject.

As I sit here today in my wheelchair I am looking ahead to some good fishing this summer. It is raining outside but I can see the lightening sky in the west, full of hope and beauty.

Postscript

ATIENTS IN F1 were from all classes and walks of life. But the majority were working people from Yorkshire who had had an accident down the pit, at work or in/on a vehicle that crashed. Almost everyone was in one of the four main public sections of F1. There was, however, a small single room on the corridor of offices and store-rooms leading into the main ward, that provided a more private bed. This was apparently (or allegedly!) reserved for people who were either rich, famous, titled, or sufficiently important (a top politician, for example) to merit the privacy of the 'single bedder'. When Sue Masham (Lady Masham, House of Lords) came in for a short spell, that was where she went.

Roger Spoor was admitted to F1 when I had already been an in-patient there for several months. Someone said he had tumbled from a balcony whilst staying at a hotel, and damaged his spine. Information (or hearsay) about the new arrival travelled fast, and in a short time there was specu-lation (or gossip) to the effect that the new arrival was "... a barrister or an accountant or summat ..."

For his first few days, as I recall, Roger was placed in the section known as 'Centre Beds', where newly injured patients were sensibly kept under close observation to allow senior staff to determine the precise prognosis, the patient's immediate needs, and then, as things stabilised, their specific medical and rehabilitation requirements. A new patient needed careful handling during this period – both physically and emotionally – and some arrivals were quite ill, or confused. Depression could set in, as the truth vaguely dawned about the implications of what had happened.

Those whose spinal injury was clearly less severe tended to weigh things up more optimistically that those whose spine had suffered a total, high level lesion. Everything was relative, as already stated.

Before long, Roger was moved to the single-bed room, giving rise to further speculation: "That new bloke's gone in the snobs' room. Must be rich or important, then." This was not meant unkindly, but reflected an attitude to class, status, or whatever, in a mainly working-class environ-ment.

We didn't see much of Roger during his first week or so, though I, along with most of the mobile patients, had nodded a brief 'hello' through his open door as we passed by. In due course he emerged, in a wheelchair, into the main part of the ward, just in time for lunch, to join the rest of us round the large table, and greeted us with: "Hello. I'm Roger Spoor. Nice to meet you."

His accent was not exactly broad Yorkshire, but rather the well modulated 'Queen's English' as spoken by BBC news readers. There were a few nods and words of welcome. Pleasantries were exchanged over lunch. "Talks a bit posh," said someone later. "Aye, well 'e would do," said another.

But a spinal injury is a great leveller, and by showing the same determination as everyone else, and the same willingness to 'muck in' and participate in the gym, at meal times, across a table tennis table or in conversation, Roger was quickly accepted. One incident that I recall quite vividly illustrates this. Ex-patients who popped in to F1 on a regular basis included some paraplegic athletes whose prowess at sports was well known. Frank Taylor (sadly no longer with us) used to roll in several times a week. Shortly after Roger's emergence into the daytime routines and banter of the main ward, he invited Frank to accompany him to his single room for an evening drink. My recollection is of Frank re-emerging an hour or two later, and announcing to all and sundry that he had just helped Roger get through a bottle of something stiff and potent. This brief announcement was followed by, "He's OK, is that Roger. Take my word for it. He's a good bloke. I know." So that settled it.

But by this time I had already begun to form a good friendship of my own with Roger, having discovered some useful common interests, such as chess, crosswords and possibly the fact that as a university student I had a more-or-less parallel academic background, with whatever that entails in terms of books read, films seen and so on. Actually, I was not much good at chess, but when the two of you are doing a standing exercise using callipers, at either end of a set of parallel bars, for an hour or more, a chess board set up on a short plank running across the bars between us, helped to pass the time! Anyway, we got on very well.

Roger fitted in well, mixing easily, displaying some mean skills at table tennis and a bit of an eye for archery. The fact that he "talked a bit posh", had a job that clearly signified ability and academic achievement, and resided in the single-bedder, were irrelevant (and rightly so) when it came to things like comradeship and participation. Roger was liked for being a good bloke who was easy to get on with, who took an honest interest in other people and had a sense of humour.

He was discharged from F1 before me, but since my discharge our friendship has continued through to the present, through the simple and sensible mechanism of exchanging Christmas cards, each one accompanied by a letter containing news as well as good wishes. This minor ritual may seem a rather slender thread, since we have not actually met since about 1971, but the strength lies in the continuity and sincerity, not in the frequency of contact.

Roger has kept me informed, down the years, about his career, the fund-raising for Kielder Adventure Centre, and his travels. My own career, in Greater Manchester, in youth and community work, has involved working with and for young disabled people, several of whom have benefited hugely from trips to places like Kielder. So in very different ways we have both been part of a wider process of empowerment and participation for disabled or disadvantaged groups in society.

David Rogers